United States Government Accountability Office

Report to Congressional Requesters

July 2012

DATA CENTER CONSOLIDATION

Agencies Making Progress on Efforts, but Inventories and Plans Need to Be Completed

GAO
Accountability ★ Integrity ★ Reliability

DATA CENTER CONSOLIDATION

Agencies Making Progress on Efforts, but Inventories and Plans Need to Be Completed

GAO

Accountability * Integrity * Reliability

Highlights

Highlights of GAO-12-742, a report to congressional requesters

Why GAO Did This Study

In 2010, as focal point for information technology management across the government, OMB's Federal Chief Information Officer launched the Federal Data Center Consolidation Initiative—an effort to consolidate the growing number of federal data centers. In July 2011, GAO evaluated 24 agencies' progress on this effort and reported that most agencies had not yet completed data center inventories or consolidation plans and recommended that they do so.

In this subsequent review, GAO was asked to (1) evaluate the extent to which the 24 agencies updated and verified their data center inventories and plans, (2) evaluate the extent to which selected agencies have adequately completed key elements of their consolidation plans, and (3) identify agencies' notable consolidation successes and challenges. To address these objectives, GAO assessed the completeness of agency inventories and plans, analyzed the schedule and cost estimates of 5 agencies previously reported to have completed one or both estimates, and interviewed officials from all 24 agencies about their consolidation successes and challenges.

What GAO Recommends

OMB's Federal Chief Information Officer should ensure that agencies use a standardized cost model to improve consolidation planning, and the 5 selected agencies should implement recognized best practices when establishing schedules and cost estimates for their consolidation efforts. OMB and 3 agencies agreed with, and 2 did not agree or disagree with, GAO's recommendations.

View GAO-12-742. For more information, contact David Powner at (202) 512-9286 or pownerd@gao.gov.

What GAO Found

As of the most recent agency data submitted in September 2011, 24 agencies identified almost 2,900 total centers, established plans to close 1,186 of them by 2015, and estimated they would realize over $2.4 billion in cost savings in doing so. However, while the Office of Management and Budget (OMB) required agencies to complete missing elements in their data center inventories and plans by the end of September 2011, only 3 agencies submitted complete inventories and only 1 agency submitted a complete plan. For example, in their inventories, 17 agencies do not provide full information on their information technology facilities and energy usage, and 8 provide only partial information on their servers. Further, in their consolidation plans, 13 agencies do not provide a full master program schedule and 21 agencies do not fully report their expected cost savings. Officials from several agencies reported that some of this information was unavailable at certain facilities or that the information was still being developed. In a prior report, GAO recommended that agencies complete the missing elements from their inventories and plans. Until these inventories and plans are complete, agencies will continue to be at risk of not realizing anticipated savings, improved infrastructure utilization, or energy efficiency.

OMB requires a master program schedule and a cost-benefit analysis (a type of cost estimate) as key requirements of agencies' consolidation plans, but none of the five agencies GAO reviewed had a schedule or cost estimate that was fully consistent with the four selected attributes of a properly sequenced schedule (such as having identified dependencies), or the four characteristics that form the basis of a reliable cost estimate (such as being comprehensive and well-documented). For example, the Departments of Interior and Transportation did not have schedules and the Department of Agriculture's schedule was consistent with three of four attributes. Additionally, cost estimates for the Departments of Homeland Security and Veterans Affairs were partially consistent with the four cost characteristics. In the absence of reliable schedules and estimates, these agencies are at risk of experiencing cost overruns, missed deadlines, and performance shortfalls. OMB has established a standardized cost model to aid agencies in their consolidation planning efforts, but use of the model is voluntary.

Many federal agencies reported consolidation successes. Notably, 20 agencies identified 34 areas of success, although only 3 of those areas were reported by more than 1 agency. The two most-reported successes were focusing on the benefits of key technologies and the benefits of working with other agencies and components to identify consolidation opportunities. However, agencies have continued to report a number of the same challenges that GAO first described in 2011, while other challenges are evolving. For example, 15 agencies reported continued issues with obtaining power usage information and 9 agencies reported that their organization continued to struggle with acquiring the funding required for consolidation. However, other challenges appear to be less prevalent, including challenges in identifying consolidation cost savings and meeting OMB's deadlines. Overall, 25 challenges that were reported in 2011 were no longer reported in 2012. In light of these successes and challenges, it is important for OMB to continue to provide leadership and guidance, such as—as GAO previously recommended—using the consolidation task force to monitor agencies' consolidation efforts.

_____ **United States Government Accountability Office**

Contents

Letter		1
	Background	2
	Agencies Updated Inventories and Plans, but Key Elements Are Still Missing	8
	Selected Agencies Have Incomplete Schedules and Cost Estimates	25
	Agencies Have Experienced Consolidation Successes and Continue to Report Challenges	34
	Conclusions	44
	Recommendations for Executive Action	45
	Agency Comments and Our Evaluation	46
Appendix I	Objectives, Scope, and Methodology	51
Appendix II	Assessment of Agencies' Completion of Key Consolidation Planning Elements, Arranged by Agency	55
Appendix III	Comments from the Department of Agriculture	103
Appendix IV	Comments from the Department of Homeland Security	104
Appendix V	Comments from the Department of the Interior	106
Appendix VI	Comments from the Department of Veterans Affairs	108
Appendix VII	Comments from the Department of Commerce	110
Appendix VIII	Comments from the Department of Energy	111

Appendix IX	Comments from the Department of Health and Human Services	112

Appendix X	Comments from the Department of Labor	114

Appendix XI	Comments from the National Science Foundation	115

Appendix XII	GAO Contact and Staff Acknowledgments	116

Tables

Table 1: Chief Information Officers Council Departments and Agencies Participating in FDCCI   4

Table 2: Comparison of Original and Revised Requirements for Agency Inventories and Plans   9

Table 3: Data Center Closures by Calendar Year, as of September 2011   11

Table 4: OMB Guidance on Key Elements of Agencies' Updated Data Center Inventories   13

Table 5: OMB Guidance on Key Elements of Agencies' Updated Consolidation Plans   18

Table 6: Select Attributes of Properly Sequenced Schedule Activities   26

Table 7: Assessment of Consistency of Agencies' Schedules with Attributes of a Properly Sequenced Schedule   27

Table 8: Characteristics of a High-quality and Reliable Cost Estimate   30

Table 9: Assessment of Consistency of Agencies' Cost Estimates with Best Practices   31

Table 10: Agency Consolidation Successes   35

Table 11: Reported Savings from Bureau of Indian Affairs Virtualization   36

Table 12: Challenges Encountered by Agencies in 2011 and 2012, Including Those No Longer Reported   39

Table 13: Chief Information Officers Council Departments and Agencies Participating in FDCCI   51

Table 14: Assessment of Completeness of Agriculture's Updated
Data Center Consolidation Documentation in 2010 and
2011   56
Table 15: Assessment of Completeness of Commerce's Updated
Data Center Consolidation Documentation in 2010 and
2011   58
Table 16: Assessment of Completeness of Defense's Updated Data
Center Consolidation Documentation in 2010 and 2011   60
Table 17: Assessment of Completeness of Education's Updated
Data Center Consolidation Documentation in 2010 and
2011   62
Table 18: Assessment of Completeness of Energy's Updated Data
Center Consolidation Documentation in 2010 and 2011   64
Table 19: Assessment of Completeness of HHS's Updated Data
Center Consolidation Documentation in 2010 and 2011   66
Table 20: Assessment of Completeness of DHS's Updated Data
Center Consolidation Documentation in 2010 and 2011   68
Table 21: Assessment of Completeness of HUD's Updated Data
Center Consolidation Documentation in 2010 and 2011   70
Table 22: Assessment of Completeness of Interior's Updated Data
Center Consolidation Documentation in 2010 and 2011   72
Table 23: Assessment of Completeness of Justice's Updated Data
Center Consolidation Documentation in 2010 and 2011   74
Table 24: Assessment of Completeness of Labor's Updated Data
Center Consolidation Documentation in 2010 and 2011   76
Table 25: Assessment of Completeness of State's Updated Data
Center Consolidation Documentation in 2010 and 2011   78
Table 26: Assessment of Completeness of Transportation's Updated
Data Center Consolidation Documentation in 2010 and 2011   80
Table 27: Assessment of Completeness of Treasury's Updated Data
Center Consolidation Documentation in 2010 and 2011   82
Table 28: Assessment of Completeness of VA's Updated Data
Center Consolidation Documentation in 2010 and 2011   84
Table 29: Assessment of Completeness of EPA's Updated Data
Center Consolidation Documentation in 2010 and 2011   86
Table 30: Assessment of Completeness of GSA's Updated Data
Center Consolidation Documentation in 2010 and 2011   88
Table 31: Assessment of Completeness of NASA's Updated Data
Center Consolidation Documentation in 2010 and 2011   90
Table 32: Assessment of Completeness of NSF's Updated Data
Center Consolidation Documentation in 2010 and 2011   92

Table 33: Assessment of Completeness of NRC's Updated Data
    Center Consolidation Documentation in 2010 and 2011   94
Table 34: Assessment of Completeness of OPM's Updated Data
    Center Consolidation Documentation in 2010 and 2011   96
Table 35: Assessment of Completeness of SBA's Updated Data
    Center Consolidation Documentation in 2010 and 2011   98
Table 36: Assessment of Completeness of SSA's Updated Data
    Center Consolidation Documentation in 2010 and 2011   100
Table 37: Assessment of Completeness of USAID's Updated Data
    Center Consolidation Documentation in 2010 and 2011   102

Figures

Figure 1: Twenty-one Agencies' Completion of Required
    Information for Data Center Inventory Key Elements, as
    of June 2011   15
Figure 2: Twenty-four Agencies' Completion of Required
    Information for Data Center Consolidation Plan Key
    Elements, as of September 2011   19

Abbreviations

CIO	chief information officer
DHS	Department of Homeland Security
EPA	Environmental Protection Agency
FDCCI	Federal Data Center Consolidation Initiative
GSA	General Services Administration
HHS	Department of Health and Human Services
HUD	Department of Housing and Urban Development
IT	information technology
NASA	National Aeronautics and Space Administration
NRC	Nuclear Regulatory Commission
NSF	National Science Foundation
OMB	Office of Management and Budget
OPM	Office of Personnel Management
SBA	Small Business Administration
SSA	Social Security Administration
TCO	total cost of ownership
USAID	U.S. Agency for International Development
VA	Department of Veterans Affairs

July 19, 2012

Congressional Requesters

The federal government's demand for information technology (IT) is ever increasing. In recent years, as federal agencies modernized their operations, put more of their services online, and increased their information security profiles, they have demanded more computing power and data storage resources. Over time, this increasing demand has led to a dramatic rise in the number of federal data centers and a corresponding increase in operational costs. The Office of Management and Budget's (OMB) Federal Chief Information Officer (CIO) has recognized the significance of this increase and in 2010, launched the Federal Data Center Consolidation Initiative (FDCCI), a governmentwide effort to consolidate data centers. In July 2011, we reported on 24 participating departments' and agencies' (agencies) progress on this effort, noting that most agencies had not yet completed the data center inventories or consolidation plans needed to implement their consolidation initiatives.[1] We recommended agencies take steps to complete the missing elements from their inventories and plans.

Given the importance of the consolidation initiative, this report responds to your request that we review the federal government's ongoing efforts to consolidate data centers. Specifically, our objectives were to (1) evaluate the extent to which agencies have updated and verified their data center inventories and consolidation plans; (2) evaluate the extent to which selected agencies have adequately completed key elements of their consolidation plans; and (3) identify agencies' notable consolidation successes and challenges.

To address our objectives, we once again assessed the 24 agencies that were identified by OMB and the Federal CIO to be included in the FDCCI initiative. We reviewed the 24 agencies' most recent data center inventories and consolidation plans and assessed their completeness against key elements required by OMB. We selected 5 agencies that had previously reported completing cost and/or schedule estimates and

---

[1]GAO, *Data Center Consolidation: Agencies Need to Complete Inventories and Plans to Achieve Expected Savings*, GAO-11-565 (Washington, D.C.: July 19, 2011).

compared these agencies' program scheduling and cost estimating documentation to best practices in program scheduling and cost estimating.[2] Finally, we reviewed all 24 agencies' documentation and interviewed agency officials to determine what consolidation successes have been realized and what challenges continue to be faced.

We conducted this performance audit from September 2011 to July 2012 in accordance with generally accepted government auditing standards. Those standards require that we plan and perform the audit to obtain sufficient, appropriate evidence to provide a reasonable basis for our findings and conclusions based on our audit objectives. We believe that the evidence obtained provides a reasonable basis for our findings and conclusions based on our audit objectives. Appendix I contains further details about our objectives, scope, and methodology.

Background

While the term "data center" can be used to describe any room used for the purpose of processing or storing data, as defined by OMB in 2010, a data center was a room greater than 500 square feet, used for processing or storing data, and which met stringent availability requirements.[3] Other facilities were classified as "server rooms," which were typically less than 500 square feet and "server closets," which were typically less than 200 square feet.

Several factors led OMB to urge agencies to consolidate federal data centers. According to OMB, the federal government had 432 data centers in 1998; more than 1,100 in 2009; and 2,094 in July 2010. Operating such a large number of centers places costly demands on the government. While the total annual federal spending associated with data centers has not yet been determined, OMB has found that operating data centers is a significant cost to the federal government, including hardware, software, real estate, and cooling costs. For example, according to the Environmental Protection Agency (EPA), the electricity cost to operate federal servers and data centers across the government is about $450

---

[2]GAO, *GAO Schedule Assessment Guide: Best Practices for Project Schedules (Exposure Draft)*, GAO-12-120G (Washington, D.C.: May 2012) and *GAO Cost Estimating and Assessment Guide*, GAO-09-3SP (Washington, D.C.: March 2009).

[3]For more information on the classifications used to define availability requirements, see Uptime Institute, *Industry Standard Tier Classifications Define Site Infrastructure Performance* (Santa Fe, N.Mex.: 2005).

million annually. According to the Department of Energy (Energy), data center spaces can consume 100 to 200 times as much electricity as standard office spaces. Reported server utilization rates as low as 5 percent and limited reuse of these data centers within or across agencies lends further credence to the need to restructure federal data center operations to improve efficiency and reduce costs. In 2010, the Federal CIO reported that operating and maintaining such redundant infrastructure investments was costly, inefficient, and unsustainable.

OMB and the Federal CIO Established the Federal Data Center Consolidation Initiative

Concerned about the size of the federal data center inventory and the potential to improve the efficiency, performance, and environmental footprint of federal data center activities, in February 2010 OMB, under the direction of the Federal CIO, announced FDCCI. This initiative's four high-level goals are to

- promote the use of "green IT"[4] by reducing the overall energy and real estate footprint of government data centers;

- reduce the cost of data center hardware, software, and operations;

- increase the overall IT security posture of the government; and

- shift IT investments to more efficient computing platforms and technologies.

As part of FDCCI, OMB required 24 departments and agencies that participate on the Chief Information Officers Council (see table 1) to submit a series of documents that ultimately resulted in a data center consolidation plan.

---

[4]"Green IT" refers to environmentally sound computing practices that can include a variety of efforts, such as using energy efficient data centers, purchasing computers that meet certain environmental standards, and recycling obsolete electronics.

Table 1: Chief Information Officers Council Departments and Agencies Participating in FDCCI

Departments	Agencies
Agriculture	Environmental Protection Agency
Commerce	General Services Administration
Defense	National Aeronautics and Space Administration
Education	National Science Foundation
Energy	Nuclear Regulatory Commission
Health and Human Services	Office of Personnel Management
Homeland Security	Small Business Administration
Housing and Urban Development	Social Security Administration
Interior	U.S. Agency for International Development
Justice	
Labor	
State	
Transportation	
Treasury	
Veterans Affairs	

Source: GAO analysis of OMB data.

In addition to an initial data center inventory and preliminary consolidation plan, the departments and agencies were to provide the following:

- An asset inventory baseline, which was to contain more detailed information and serve as the foundation for developing the final data center consolidation plans. The final inventory was also to identify the consolidation approach to be taken for each data center.

- A data center consolidation plan, which was to be incorporated into the agency's fiscal year 2012 budget and was to include a technical roadmap and approach for achieving the targets for infrastructure utilization, energy efficiency, and cost efficiency.

In October 2010, OMB reported that all of the agencies had submitted their plans. OMB also announced plans to monitor agencies' consolidation activities on an ongoing basis as part of the annual budget process.

Further, starting in fiscal year 2011, agencies were required to provide an annual updated data center asset inventory at the end of every third quarter and an updated consolidation plan (including any missing elements) at the end of every fourth quarter. Agencies were further required to provide a consolidation progress report at the end of every quarter.

GAO-12-742 Data Center Consolidation

To manage the initiative, OMB designated two agency CIOs as executive sponsors to lead the effort within the Chief Information Officers Council.[5] Additionally, the General Services Administration (GSA) has established the FDCCI Program Management Office, whose role is to support OMB in the planning, execution, management, and communication for FDCCI. In this role, GSA collected the responses to OMB-mandated document deliveries and reviewed the submissions for completeness and reasonableness. GSA also sponsored three workshops on the initiative for agencies and facilitated a peer review of the initial and final data center consolidation plans.

With an Expanded Definition, OMB's Reported Inventory of Federal Data Centers Has Grown

OMB has utilized different definitions of a data center throughout the life of FDCCI. As discussed earlier, OMB originally defined these facilities as rooms that met certain size, purpose, and availability requirements. So, even though agencies included smaller facilities (such as server rooms and closets) in their inventories, these facilities were not included in the data center tallies. However, in October 2011, the Federal CIO announced an expansion of the definition to include facilities of any size. Using this broader definition, in December 2011, OMB reported that there were 3,133 federal data centers.[6] OMB further clarified its definition in March 2012 as follows:

> "...a data center is...a closet, room, floor or building for the storage, management, and dissemination of data and information and [used to house] computer systems and associated components, such as database, application, and storage systems and data stores [excluding facilities exclusively devoted to communications and network equipment (e.g., telephone exchanges and telecommunications rooms)]. A data center generally includes redundant or backup power supplies, redundant data communications connections, environmental controls...and special security devices housed in leased,...owned, collocated, or stand-alone facilities."[7]

---

[5] As of May 2012, one of the CIOs was from the Department of the Interior (Interior). As of July 2012, OMB was currently working to fill the second position.

[6] OMB's reported tally of data centers differs from the number of data centers we found in reviewing agencies' June 2011 inventories and September 2011 consolidation goals. The number of centers changes regularly as agencies identify new centers, but agencies are only required to provide updated inventories once a year, by the end of June.

[7] OMB, *Implementation Guidance for the Federal Data Center Consolidation Initiative* (Washington, D.C.: Mar. 19, 2012).

OMB's IT Reform Plan Sets Important Milestones for Data Center Consolidation

In December 2010, OMB published its *25-Point Implementation Plan to Reform Federal Information Technology Management* as a means of implementing IT reform in the areas of operational efficiency and large scale IT program management. Among the 25 initiatives, OMB has included two goals that relate to data center consolidation:

1. By June 2011, complete detailed implementation plans to consolidate at least 800 data centers by 2015.

2. By June 2012, create a governmentwide marketplace for data center availability.

To accomplish its first goal, OMB required each FDCCI agency to identify a senior, dedicated data center consolidation program manager. It also launched a Data Center Consolidation Task Force comprised of the data center consolidation program managers from each agency. OMB officials stated that this task force is critical to driving forward on individual agency consolidation goals and to meeting overall federal consolidation targets. OMB has also created a publicly available dashboard for observing agencies' consolidation progress.

To accomplish its second goal, OMB and GSA launched a governmentwide data center availability marketplace in June 2012. This online marketplace is intended to match agencies that have extra capacity with agencies with increasing demand, thereby improving the utilization of existing facilities. The marketplace will help agencies with available capacity promote their available data center space. Once agencies have a clear sense of the existing capacity landscape, they can make more informed consolidation decisions.

GAO Has Previously Reported on Federal Data Center Consolidation Efforts

We have previously reported on OMB's efforts to consolidate federal data centers. In March 2011, we reported on the status of the FDCCI and noted that data center consolidation makes sense economically and is a way to achieve more efficient IT operations, but that challenges exist.[8] For example, agencies reported facing challenges in ensuring the accuracy of their inventories and plans, providing upfront funding for the

---

[8]GAO, *Opportunities to Reduce Potential Duplication in Government Programs, Save Tax Dollars, and Enhance Revenue*, GAO-11-318SP (Washington, D.C.: Mar. 1, 2011).

consolidation effort before any cost savings accrue, integrating consolidation plans into agency budget submissions (as required by OMB), establishing and implementing shared standards (for storage, systems, security, etc.), overcoming cultural resistance to such major organizational changes, and maintaining current operations during the transition to consolidated operations. We further reported that mitigating these and other challenges will require commitment from the agencies and continued oversight by OMB and the Federal CIO.

In July 2011, we reported that agency consolidation plans indicate that agencies anticipated closing about 650 data centers by fiscal year 2015 and saving about $700 million in doing so.[9] However, we also found that only one of the 24 agencies submitted a complete inventory and no agency submitted complete plans. Further, OMB did not require agencies to document the steps they took, if any, to verify the inventory data. We noted the importance of having assurance as to the accuracy of collected data and specifically, the need for agencies to provide OMB with complete and accurate data and the possible negative impact of that data being missing or incomplete. We concluded that until these inventories and plans are complete, agencies may not be able to implement their consolidation activities and realize expected cost savings. Moreover, without an understanding of the validity of agencies' consolidation data, OMB could not be assured that agencies are providing a sound baseline for estimating consolidation savings and measuring progress against those goals. Accordingly, we made several recommendations to OMB, including that the Federal CIO require that agencies, when updating their data center inventories, state what actions have been taken to verify the inventories and to identify any associated limitations on the data. We also recommended that the Federal CIO require that agencies complete the missing elements in their consolidation plans and in doing so, consider consolidation challenges and lessons learned. We also made recommendations to the heads of agencies to complete the information missing from their inventories and plans.

In response to our recommendations, OMB took several actions. Beginning in fiscal year 2011, in addition to the updated inventories due at the end of every third fiscal quarter, agencies are required to submit an updated consolidation plan by the end of every fourth fiscal quarter. Along

---

[9]GAO-11-565.

with the updated plan, agencies are required to submit a signed letter from their CIOs, attesting to the completeness of the plan, stating what actions were taken to verify the inventory, and noting any limitations of inventory or plan data. The inclusion of this performance information will continue to be important to OMB as it makes decisions on how best to oversee the ongoing federal data center consolidations. By gathering this understanding of the validity and limitation on agencies' data, OMB will be better assured that agencies are providing a sound baseline for estimating savings and accurately reporting progress against their goals. The extent to which agencies have completed information missing from their inventories and plans is discussed in the following section.

More recently, in February 2012, we updated our March 2011 work and reported that although OMB had taken steps to ensure the completion of agencies' consolidation plans, a preliminary analysis indicated that not all plans were complete.[10] Also, in April 2012, we reported on the progress OMB and federal agencies made in implementing the IT Reform Plan, including one action item associated with data center consolidation.[11] We reported that this goal was only partially completed, based on our conclusion that not all of the agencies' updated data center consolidation plans included the required elements.

Agencies Updated Inventories and Plans, but Key Elements Are Still Missing

As discussed earlier, OMB required agencies to submit an updated data center inventory that included information on each center and its assets by the end of June 2011, and an updated consolidation plan that included key information on the agencies' consolidation approach by the end of September 2011. OMB subsequently issued revised guidance on the mandatory content of the data center inventories and consolidation plans, in May 2011 and July 2011, respectively. While the revised inventory guidance asked for different information from what was requested in 2010, it still required agencies to report on specific assets within individual data centers, as well as information about each specific data center. The revised guidance on consolidation plans was similar to the 2010

---

[10]GAO, *Follow-up on 2011 Report: Status of Actions Taken to Address Duplication, Overlap, and Fragmentation, Save Tax Dollars, and Enhance Revenue*, GAO-12-453SP (Washington, D.C.: Feb. 28, 2012).

[11]GAO, *Information Technology Reform: Progress Made; More Needs to Be Done to Complete Actions and Measure Results*, GAO-12-461 (Washington, D.C.: Apr. 26, 2012).

GAO-12-742 Data Center Consolidation

guidance, but included several additional requirements. Specifically, in addition to continuing to require information on key elements such as goals, approaches, schedules, cost-benefit calculations, and risk management plans, the revised guidance also required agencies to address the data verification steps, consolidation progress, and cost savings. Table 2 compares the original and revised requirements for key elements to be included in agency inventories and plans.

Table 2: Comparison of Original and Revised Requirements for Agency Inventories and Plans

2010 inventory elements	2011 inventory elements
IT software assets	[Deleted]
IT hardware and utilization	Physical servers[a]
	Virtualization[b]
IT facilities, energy, and storage	IT facilities, energy
	Network storage
Geographic location	Data center information
2010 plan elements	**2011 plan elements**
Quantitative goals	Quantitative goals
Qualitative impacts	Qualitative impacts
Consolidation approach	Consolidation approach
Consolidation scope	Consolidation scope
High-level timeline	High-level timeline
Performance metrics	Performance metrics
Master program schedule	Master program schedule
Cost-benefit analysis	Cost-benefit analysis
Risk management	Risk management
Communications plan	Communications plan
	Inventory/plan verification
	Consolidation progress
	Cost savings

Source: GAO analysis of OMB data.

[a]The term "physical server" refers to a physical piece of hardware that can be used to run multiple software-based virtual machines with different operating systems in isolation and side-by-side. OMB captures information about such software-based virtual machines in the category called "virtualization."

[b]"Virtualization" is a technology that allows multiple, software-based machines, with different operating systems, to run in isolation, side-by-side, on the same physical machine.

While all agencies submitted updated inventories and plans in 2011, most of the agencies' documents are still not complete. As required, all 24 agencies[12] submitted their inventories in June 2011 and all but 2 submitted their updated consolidation plans in September 2011. The Social Security Administration (SSA) submitted its updated consolidation plan in October 2011 and the Department of Defense (Defense) submitted an updated consolidation plan in November 2011. However, of the 24 agencies' submissions, only 3 of the inventories are complete and only 1 of the plans is complete. For example, while all 24 agencies report on their inventories to some extent, 8 agencies provide only partial information on the new category of physical servers and 17 provide only partial information on the new category of IT facilities and energy usage. Additionally, in their consolidation plans, 13 agencies do not provide a full master program schedule, 17 agencies do not provide full cost-benefit analysis results, and 21 agencies do not include all required cost savings information. In the absence of important information such as schedules and cost estimates, agencies are at risk of not realizing key FDCCI goals such as anticipated cost savings and improved infrastructure utilization.

Agencies Continue to Report Significant Planned Facility Reductions and Cost Savings

While agencies' inventories and goals have changed since we last reported on FDCCI, agencies continue to report plans to significantly reduce the number of their centers and to achieve cost savings. Last year, we reported that as of April 2011, 23 agencies identified 1,590 centers (using the large data center definition) and established goals to reduce that number by 652. Our most recent analysis of 24 agencies' documentation indicates that as of September 2011, agencies identified almost 2,900 total centers, and established plans to close over 1,185 of them by 2015. The new total number of data centers includes 648 large centers (500 square feet or more), 1,283 smaller centers (less than 500 square feet), and 966 centers of undetermined size.[13] The centers of undetermined size are primarily comprised of 936 Defense facilities, a list of which was provided in a format that did not allow for an analysis of the

---

[12]In GAO-11-565, we reported that one agency, the Department of Housing and Urban Development (HUD), did not submit the required consolidation documentation. However, the department has now submitted both an inventory and plan.

[13]As noted earlier, SSA and Defense did not meet the September deadline for their inventories. Thus, the SSA data are as of October 2011 and the Defense data are as of November 2011.

size of the centers.[14] An OMB official attributed the change in the number of large centers reported to agencies' improvements in data quality.[15]

Table 3 contains a further breakdown of actual and planned closures by calendar year, for both large and smaller centers.

Table 3: Data Center Closures by Calendar Year, as of September 2011

	Total centers	Closures by calendar year					
		Through 2011	2012	2013	2014	2015	Total
Large centers (≥500 square feet)	648	89	81	43	75	21	309
Smaller centers (<500 square feet)	1,283	58	124	73	25	23	303
Centers of unknown classification	966	139	141	96	116	82	574
Total	**2,897**	**286**	**346**	**212**	**216**	**126**	**1,186**

Source: GAO analysis of agency data.

Note: OMB required agencies to report planned closures by calendar year in both the June 2011 inventory and September 2011 consolidation plan updates. However, several agencies reported planned closures on a fiscal year basis. We have attempted, where possible, to convert such information into the correct calendar year, but this was not always possible. As a result, the annual totals may differ slightly from the true targets.

The number of facilities in agencies' inventories has changed over time, and will likely continue to evolve. For example, in July 2011, we reported that agencies reported having 1,590 large centers in their inventories, whereas they now report only 648. There are multiple reasons for these fluctuations. Some agencies have reported confusion over the evolving definition of "data center," while officials from other agencies told us that

---

[14]In 2011, we reported that Defense had 772 large centers, but that number could not be confirmed in the department's latest inventory. In May 2012, a Defense official reported that of the 936 reported Defense facilities, 645 fit our definition of "large data centers." However, this number was not provided in time to be validated for this report and the official did not break the number down into closures by calendar year. As such, Defense's data centers are only reported under the unknown classification category.

[15]In May 2012, the Energy Office of Inspector General reported that the department had not reported more than 520 data centers at contractor-operated locations. U.S. Department of Energy, Office of Inspector General, *Efforts by the Department of Energy to Ensure Energy-Efficient Management of Its Data Centers*, DOE/IG-0865 (Washington, D.C.: May 25, 2012).

some facilities have been reclassified or dropped from the inventory as more was learned about the facilities. Additionally, agencies have reported that their inventory totals are in a constant state of flux and changing on a regular basis as a result of their efforts to gather and refine information about data center inventories.

Most agencies also continued to report expected savings from FDCCI. Specifically,

- Nineteen agencies reported anticipating more than $2.4 billion in cost savings and more than $820 million in cost avoidances, between 2011 and 2015.[16] Additionally, as we also reported in 2011, actual savings may be even higher because 14 of these agencies' projections were incomplete.[17]

- One agency does not expect to accrue net savings until 2017.

- One agency does not expect to attain net savings from its consolidation efforts.

- Three agencies did not provide estimated cost savings.

While we recognize that agencies' planned savings of over $2.4 billion may grow as agencies complete their cost and savings assessments, the President's budget for fiscal year 2013 states that FDCCI is expected to realize $3 billion in savings by 2015.[18] This reflects a $600 million dollar disparity between what agencies are reporting and what OMB is expecting. Such a disparity highlights the need for agencies to continue to develop and refine their savings projections, in order to make clear an accurate picture of the goals to be realized by the governmentwide consolidation initiative.

---

[16]OMB defines cost savings as representing a reduction in actual expenditures to achieve a specific objective. The agency defines cost avoidances as results from an action taken in the immediate time frame that will decrease costs in the future.

[17]GAO-11-565.

[18]OMB, *Analytical Perspectives, Budget of the U.S. Government, Fiscal Year 2013* (Washington, D.C.: Feb. 13, 2012).

Asset Inventories Are Still Not Complete

In our July 2011 report, we recommended that agencies complete the missing elements from their inventories. Further, as part of FDCCI, OMB required agencies to update their data center inventories at the end of the third quarter of every fiscal year. In guidance provided to the agencies, the 2011 updated inventories were to address five key elements for each data center: (1) physical servers, (2) virtualization, (3) IT facilities and energy, (4) network storage, and (5) data center information. One information category from 2010, IT software assets, was no longer required. Table 4 provides a detailed description of each of the five key elements.

Table 4: OMB Guidance on Key Elements of Agencies' Updated Data Center Inventories

Element	Guidance
Physical servers	The inventory should document the current rack count[a] and the number of mainframes and servers in each facility.
Virtualization	The inventory should document the virtual host count and virtual operating system count for each facility.[b]
IT facilities and energy	The inventory should document each facility's power capacity, electricity usage, electricity cost, and whether the facility's electricity is metered.
Network storage	The inventory should document each facility's total storage capacity and utilization.
Data center information	The inventory should document each facility's data center tier/type, size, cost (including whether electricity is included), consolidation status, and information on the number and cost of full-time employees at the facility.

Source: GAO analysis of OMB data.

[a]A rack is a physical structure used to house computer servers.

[b]Virtual hosts and virtual operating systems are software-based machines and tools that can run in isolation, side-by-side, on the same physical machine.

However, not all of the agencies used the revised format. Specifically, 21 of the 24 agencies submitted inventories in OMB's updated format and 3 agencies (the Department of Agriculture (Agriculture), the Office of Personnel Management (OPM), and the Small Business Administration (SBA)) used the former format.[19] Officials from all 3 agencies stated that they thought they were using the correct format at the time. Further, these

---

[19]Because the 2010 and 2011 formats differ to the extent that they cannot be appropriately compared, the status of those three inventories is not reported here. However, an assessment of their inventories can be found in the detailed agency discussions in app. II.

GAO-12-742 Data Center Consolidation

officials said they plan to submit information consistent with OMB's revised inventory template in the future.

The confusion by selected agencies on which templates to use is due, in part, to a change in how OMB distributed its new guidance. While in prior years the Federal CIO wrote letters to agency CIOs and OMB posted its guidance on the FDCCI website, in conveying the direction to use a new template in spring 2011, the Federal CIO did not write letters to agency CIOs and OMB did not post its latest guidance online. Instead, the Federal CIO and OMB relied on more informal means, such as the FDCCI task force meetings, to disseminate the new guidance. Although the task force serves as an important communications conduit for FDCCI, the confusion we identified among agencies on which template to use demonstrates that the task force was not effective as the sole means of communication with the agencies. In providing guidance and direction, task force communications could be enhanced by leveraging other existing resources, such as sending letters from the Federal CIO to agency CIOs and posting the guidance on the initiative's website.

In assessing agencies' inventories, we rated an element as complete if the agency provided all of the information required for the element, partial if the agency provided some, but not all, of the information for the element, and incomplete if the agency did not provide the information required for the element. A partial rating could result if an agency did not provide any information for selected facilities or if the agency did not fill in selected fields for its facilities. For example, both an agency providing data on two of five facilities and an agency providing incomplete data on energy usage across facilities would receive partial ratings.

Of the 21 inventories in the new format, only 3 contain complete data for all five of the required elements. Additionally, while all agencies provide at least partial inventory data for all five elements,

- one agency provides complete information for four of the five elements,

- eight agencies provide complete information for three of the five elements,

- three agencies provide complete information for two of the five elements,

- two agencies provide complete information for one of the five elements, and

- four agencies do not have any complete elements in their inventories.

Figure 1 provides an assessment of the completeness of agencies' inventories, by key element, and a discussion of the analysis of each element follows the figure. In addition, a detailed summary of each agency's completion of key elements is provided in appendix II.

Figure 1: Twenty-one Agencies' Completion of Required Information for Data Center Inventory Key Elements, as of June 2011

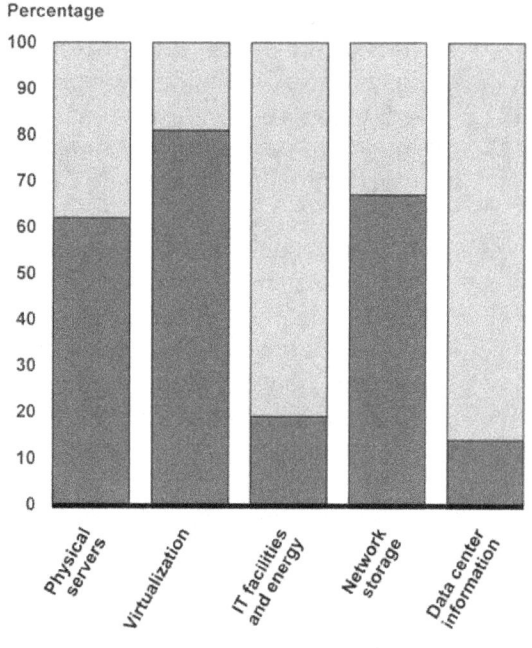

Percentage

No – the agency does not provide information for this inventory element

Partial – the agency provides some, but not all, of the information for this inventory element

Yes – the agency provides complete information for this inventory element

Source: GAO analysis of agency data.

- **Physical servers.** Thirteen agencies provide complete information on their physical servers and 8 agencies provide partial information. For example, the Department of Education (Education) provides complete information on its total rack count and counts of types of servers, while the Department of Health and Human Services (HHS) provides complete counts of individual servers, but partial information on total rack count. Additionally, the Department of Justice (Justice) provides partial information for both its total rack count and types of servers.

- **Virtualization.** Seventeen agencies provide complete information on their virtualization and 4 agencies provide partial information. For example, HUD, the Departments of State (State) and Veterans Affairs (VA), and the National Science Foundation (NSF), all provide complete information on their virtual host count and virtual operating system count. In contrast, the Departments of Defense, Homeland Security (DHS), Justice, and GSA provide partial information for both of those same elements.

- **IT facilities and energy.** Four agencies provide complete information on their IT facilities and energy, while 17 provide partial information. For example, the Nuclear Regulatory Commission (NRC) and SSA fully provide such information as total data center power capacity and average data center electricity usage. However, VA fully reports on total data center power capacity, but partially on average data center electricity usage and total IT data center power capacity. Further, the Department of Labor (Labor) partially reports on total data center IT power capacity and average data center electricity usage and does not report any information on total data center power capacity.

- **Network storage.** Fourteen agencies provide complete information on their network storage and 7 provide partial information. For example, the Departments of Commerce (Commerce) and Transportation (Transportation), EPA, the National Aeronautics and Space Administration (NASA), and the U.S. Agency for International Development (USAID) all fully report on their total and used network storage. Other agencies, such as Defense, HHS, and State partially report information in each of those two categories.

- **Data center information.** Three agencies provide complete information on their individual data centers, while 18 provide partial information. For example, HUD and SSA both fully report on data center-specific information such as data center type, gross floor area, and target date for closure. Other agencies, such as Energy and VA fully report on gross floor area and closure information, but partially report data center costs. Also, agencies such as Defense and DHS report partial information in all categories.

Part of the reason the agencies' inventories remain incomplete stems from challenges in gathering data center power information, a key component of the IT facilities and energy component, and more broadly, problems providing good quality asset inventories, as OMB requires. These challenges are discussed in more detail later in this report. Because the continued progress of FDCCI is largely dependent on accomplishing goals built on the information provided by agency inventories, it will be important for agencies to continue to work on completing their inventories, thus providing a sound basis for their savings and utilization forecasts.

Agencies Updated Consolidation Plans, but Most Plans Are Not Complete

In addition to the agencies' inventories, we previously recommended and OMB required agencies to update their consolidation plans to address any missing elements. OMB's revised guidance on the contents of the consolidation plans retains key elements from its prior guidance and adds requirements to discuss steps taken to verify inventory and plan data, consolidation progress, and consolidation cost savings. OMB has previously reported on the importance of agencies' consolidation plans in providing a technical road map and approach for achieving specified targets for infrastructure utilization, energy efficiency, and cost efficiency. Table 5 provides a detailed description of each of these elements.

Table 5: OMB Guidance on Key Elements of Agencies' Updated Consolidation Plans

Element	Guidance
Quantitative goals	The agency should define high-level asset reduction and IT infrastructure utilization improvement goals, which include agencywide savings and utilization forecasts through fiscal year 2015. These forecasts are to address projected reductions for data centers, aggregate gross floor area, total number of racks, total number of servers, and the corresponding utilization metrics (including server virtualization percentages).
Qualitative impacts	Agency goals need to include qualitative impacts targeted by the agency (e.g., standardization, economies of scale, procurement improvements, security and operational efficiency improvements, etc.).
Summary of approach	The agency needs to include a brief summary for each of the specific approaches that will be undertaken to achieve the stated goals.
Scope of consolidation	The plan needs to include a clear, well-defined scope for implementing the FDCCI, by identifying the specific target agency/component/bureau data centers to be consolidated.
High-level timeline	The plan needs to include a high-level timeline for data center consolidation.
Performance metrics	The agency's governance framework for data center consolidation needs to include specific metrics that will be used in performance measurement.
Master program schedule	A master program schedule needs to be created for the entire agency, from the detailed implementation schedules provided by each of the data center managers as well as driven by related federal government activities (e.g., OMB reporting, budget submission, or beginning of a new fiscal year).
Cost-benefit analysis	The plan is to include a cost-benefit analysis stating, for each fiscal year included as part of the agency's final consolidation plan, aggregate year-by-year investment and cost savings calculations through fiscal year 2015.
Risk management plan	A risk management plan needs to be developed and risks need to be tracked using templates.
Communications plan	Depending on the scope and impact of the consolidation plan, the agency should consider developing a communications plan for the FDCCI implementation at the agency. Issues to consider in this communications plan include: key internal and external stakeholder needs/concerns; senior leadership briefing reports; and regular coordination with key parties involved in plan implementation.
Inventory/plan verification	The plan should describe the steps taken to verify that inventory data and the consolidation plan are complete, accurate and consistent. Also the plan should identify any significant data limitations.
Consolidation progress	The plan should document if the agency met data center consolidation targets through 9/30/11 and address whether the agency is prepared to meet calendar year 2012 targets. The plan should also highlight the agency's successes and challenges experienced to date. The plan should also consider any consolidation lessons learned.
Cost savings	The plan needs to address cost savings realized in calendar year 2011 and how those savings related to established targets. The plan should also provide what future savings will be based on 2011 efforts, whether there were any unexpected costs, and whether the agency's fiscal year 2011 enacted budget had any impact on consolidation efforts.

Source: GAO analysis of OMB data.

All 24 agencies submitted consolidation plans to OMB, but only 1 agency has a complete plan. For the remaining 23 agencies, selected elements are missing from each plan. For example, among the 24 agencies, all provide complete information on their qualitative impacts, but only 9 provide complete information on their quantitative goals. Further, 23 agencies specify their consolidation approach, but only 5 indicate that a full cost-benefit analysis was performed for the consolidation initiative. In many cases, agencies submitted some, but not all, of the required information. Figure 2 provides an assessment of the completeness of agencies' consolidation plans, by key element, and a discussion of each element follows the figure. In addition, a detailed summary of each agency's completion of key elements is provided in appendix II.

Figure 2: Twenty-four Agencies' Completion of Required Information for Data Center Consolidation Plan Key Elements, as of September 2011

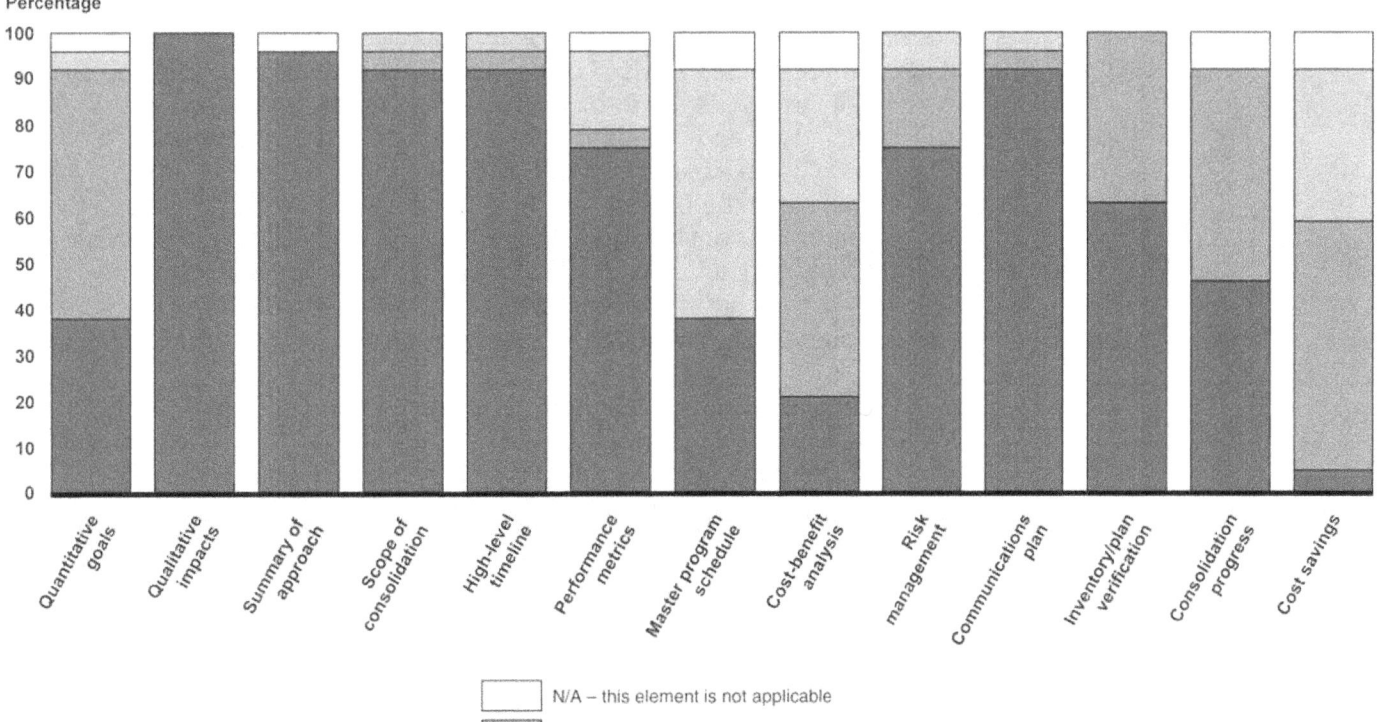

Source: GAO analysis of agency data.

- **Quantitative goals.** Nine agencies provide complete savings and utilization forecasts, 13 agencies provide partial forecasts, 1 agency does not provide any information, and an official from 1 agency said that this element did not apply. For example, Agriculture and Labor were rated as providing partial forecasts because they provide complete savings forecasts, but incomplete utilization forecasts. State and NRC were rated as providing partial forecasts because they both

GAO-12-742 Data Center Consolidation

provide incomplete savings and utilization forecasts. Some agencies identified reasons for not having completed these forecasts. Specifically, a Department of the Interior (Interior) official told us that it was not cost effective to gather the missing information, so it was not included. Officials from other agencies, such as Labor and NRC, told us of data quality problems or that their data centers lacked the ability to gather the required information. Further, a HUD official stated that the department did not have any quantitative goals because their consolidation effort was completed in 2005.

- **Qualitative impacts.** All 24 agencies fully describe the qualitative impacts of their consolidation initiatives. For example, Commerce's plan describes goals such as controlling data center costs and shifting IT investments to more efficient computing platforms and technologies. Additionally, NASA reports that the consolidation effort will provide access to cost and power-efficient data centers that will meet all of the agency's computing needs, as well as transform the data center environment, in part through virtualization and the use of cloud services. Further, SBA describes goals such as reducing the amount of physical resources consumed by technology systems and modernizing and updating agency systems.

- **Summary of consolidation approach.** Twenty-three agencies include a summary of the agencies' consolidation approaches and an official from 1 agency said that this element did not apply. For example, Defense describes the department's reference architecture for use in guiding the consolidation effort and also provides examples of how the Air Force and the Army are approaching aspects of their respective consolidations. Additionally, State's plan details how the department will consolidate all domestic data centers into four enterprise data centers. Additionally, a HUD official stated that this element was not applicable because the department's consolidation effort was completed in 2005.

- **Scope of consolidation.** Twenty-two agencies' plans include a well-defined scope for data center consolidation, 1 provides partial information on the scope of their consolidation efforts, and 1 does not provide this information. Specifically, the agencies that provide this information list the data centers included in the consolidation effort and what consolidation approach will be taken for each center. For example, EPA lists the 25 facilities for which either the servers will be moved or the site will be decommissioned. Similarly, Justice lists the 36 centers that will be either consolidated or decommissioned. However, Labor only partially addresses consolidation scope because it only provides information on about half of its data centers. According to an agency official, the centers that have been addressed constitute the bulk of the agency's computing power, but that the remaining facilities will be addressed in a later phase of the consolidation effort, the timing for which has not yet been determined. Additionally, Defense has not defined its consolidation scope. A Defense consolidation program official stated that the department was still working to better understand the full inventory for all departmental components.

- **High-level timeline.** Twenty-two agencies include a high-level timeline for consolidation efforts, 1 agency includes partial information on its timeline, and 1 does not provide a timeline. For example, Justice and EPA both provide the year for which action will be taken on their centers to be consolidated and NRC lists the years its three centers will be consolidated before they are replaced by NRC's new data center. In contrast, Labor provides a timeline for about half of its data centers, and Defense does not provide a timeline because it has not fully defined the scope of its consolidation effort.

- **Performance metrics.** Eighteen agencies identify specific performance metrics for their consolidation programs, 1 agency provides partial information on its metrics, 4 agencies do not identify specific metrics, and an official from 1 agency said that this element did not apply. Specifically, Agriculture's plan defines several key performance indicators such as the numbers of applications moved and physical servers eliminated. Additionally, several agencies, such as Commerce, Defense, and NSF, provide consolidation performance metrics based on quantitative savings and utilization goals. As an example of an agency with partial metrics, Education identifies metrics based on its savings goals, but is missing information on its progress in meeting utilization goals. Additionally, DHS and NRC do not identify any performance metrics. Officials from both DHS and NRC agreed that their agencies did not have such measures when their plans were published, but noted that the required metrics had since been developed or that they now have the resources to develop them. Further, a HUD official stated that this element was not applicable because the department's consolidation effort was completed in 2005.

- **Master program schedule.** Nine agencies reference a completed master program schedule, 13 agencies do not reference such a schedule, and officials from 2 agencies said that this element did not apply. For example, HHS, VA, and GSA discuss their master program schedules, but other agencies, such as State and EPA do not reference schedules in their plans. State officials noted that the department has a schedule, but that it was not included in their consolidation plan due to a miscommunication. They stated that it would be included in their next plan update. Some agencies, such as Defense and Labor, are working to develop their schedules or will develop them in the future. A Defense official told us that the department has drafted a combined data center consolidation and cloud computing master schedule that is expected to be approved by the end of September 2012. Officials from Energy told us that their consolidation schedule existed, but that it was part of a larger departmental effort and did not provide detail down to the individual data center level. Officials from OPM questioned the utility of a master program schedule for relatively limited consolidation efforts. Two agencies reported that this requirement was not applicable to their situation. Specifically, officials from Education stated that this requirement was not applicable because of the small scale of their agency's consolidation efforts. Additionally, a HUD official stated that this element was not applicable because the department's consolidation effort was completed in 2005.

- **Cost-benefit analysis.** Five agencies provide results from a complete cost-benefit analysis that encompasses their entire consolidation initiative, 10 agencies provide only selected elements of a cost-benefit analysis, and 7 agencies do not provide a cost-benefit analysis. This element did not apply to 2 agencies. For example, Commerce details full annualized cost and savings estimates through fiscal year 2015, while other agencies, such as HHS and Interior provide only partial information. Specifically, HHS addresses projected savings, but not costs, and Interior acknowledges that an analysis has not yet been completed. Some agencies, such as Defense and Energy, plan to complete a cost-benefit analysis in the future. Officials from Transportation told us that the department was working on a new cost-benefit analysis, as the department no longer felt comfortable with their original savings projections. An Education official noted that the department's consolidation did not cost anything and that although data will be moved out of the department's one server room to be consolidated by the end of 2012, the facility would still operate as a network center. Additionally, a HUD official stated that this element was not applicable because the department's consolidation effort was completed in 2005.

- **Risk management plan.** Eighteen agencies reference a consolidation risk management plan and require that risks be tracked, 4 agencies partially address risk management, and 2 agencies do not address risk management. For example, DHS describes its Data Center Services Project Risk Management Plan, including how risks are identified, assessed, and mitigated throughout the development life cycle. Additionally, Transportation addresses how its risk management plan identifies and tracks risks in three categories: people, process, and technology and administration. In contrast, agencies such as Energy and Interior are rated as partial because they are continuing to develop their risk management processes. An Interior official told us that the department's plan is scheduled to be completed by June 2012. Officials from both OPM and SBA acknowledged that their consolidation plans did not address a risk management plan, but noted that risk was either being managed as part of individual projects or within a larger context within their respective organizations.

- **Communications plan.** Twenty-two agencies consider a communications plan for the agencies' consolidation initiatives, 1 agency does so partially, and 1 agency does not. For example, HHS describes a series of organizational responsibilities for gathering and reporting project information, as well as communicating with other departmental stakeholders. Additionally, GSA describes how its communications approach ensures that stakeholders both within and outside of the agency are kept informed as to consolidation progress. The Department of the Treasury (Treasury) partially addresses its communications plan, noting that it is maintained as part of a larger departmental effort. OPM makes no such reference. Further, an official from OPM told us that a communications plan was not as critical for a small agency.

- **Inventory and plan verification.** Fifteen agencies fully describe the steps taken to ensure that inventories and plans were complete and accurate, and 9 agencies partially do so. For example, State describes how information was gathered and validated, addresses several limitations, and attests to the documents' completeness. Additionally, EPA describes how information was validated, describes limitations on inventory data, and attests to the currency of the agency's plans. However, other agencies, such as Agriculture, HUD, and SSA are rated as having partially completed this element because they note that information was validated, but do not address data limitations or the completeness of both the inventory and plan. A HUD official told us that the department was unaware of this requirement and agreed to consider what could be said in the next plan update. An SSA official acknowledged that this information was meant to be included, but was inadvertently omitted.

- **Consolidation progress.** Eleven agencies fully report on progress meeting consolidation goals, 11 agencies do so partially, and this element does not apply to 2 agencies. Specifically, Justice addresses progress against consolidation goals, discusses consolidation challenges, and references consolidation successes, such as integrating lessons learned from other organizations. VA similarly describes progress against goals and challenges, and also notes the department's reliance on commercial and public best practices while updating its consolidation plan. However, both Education and NASA are rated as partially completing this element because they discuss progress against goals, but do not present specific successes or challenges. A NASA official agreed that this information was not included, but stated that the agency was aware of situations that addressed both categories of information. Additionally, a HUD official stated that this element was not applicable because the department's consolidation effort was completed in 2005. OPM officials stated that the agency followed OMB's original guidance when completing their updated consolidation plan, which did not include a requirement for reporting on consolidation progress.

- **Cost savings.** Only 1 agency fully reports on consolidation cost savings, while 13 agencies do so partially, and 8 do not. This element does not apply to two other agencies. Specifically, Commerce discusses net savings, future savings, budgetary impacts, and that the consolidation effort did not incur any unexpected costs. In contrast, HHS and Justice address net and future savings, but not budgetary impacts or unexpected costs. Additionally, other agencies do not include this information for various reasons. Notably, a Defense official told us that it was challenging to gather savings information from all the department's components. An NSF official told us the information was not included because the agency had not yet realized any cost savings and so, had nothing to report. However, the agency expected to have more to report in the future. Additionally, a HUD official stated that this element was not applicable because the department's consolidation effort was completed in 2005. Further, as with reporting on consolidation progress, OPM officials stated that they followed OMB's original guidance, which did not include a requirement relating to cost savings.

In the continued absence of completed consolidation plans, agencies are at risk of implementing their respective initiatives without a clear understanding of their current state and proposed end state. For example, OMB intends for agencies' master program schedules to provide an agencywide plan drawn from detailed implementation schedules for each data center. However, only nine agencies have fully completed this activity. Further, OMB intends agencies' cost-benefit analyses to assess planned investments and cost savings calculations on a year-by-year basis, thus capturing realistic estimates of funding needed or savings realized from the closing of facilities and associated reduction in energy use. Nonetheless, only five agencies have completed such a study. Without completing this information, agencies may not realize anticipated cost savings, improved infrastructure utilization, or energy efficiency. The importance of these two practices is further discussed in the following section.

Selected Agencies Have Incomplete Schedules and Cost Estimates

OMB requires both a master program schedule and a cost-benefit analysis as key elements of agencies' consolidation plans, but none of the agencies we evaluated had complete schedules or cost estimates. A comprehensive schedule is an important foundational element for initiative planning and provides a road map for systematic project execution. A credible cost-benefit analysis, which is one type of cost estimate, is a key tool for management to use in making informed decisions and includes information such as relative benefits and the effect and value of cost trade-offs. However, of five agencies (Agriculture, DHS, Interior, Transportation, and VA) selected for further analysis, none had a schedule or cost estimate that was fully consistent with best practices. Of the five agencies, two did not have schedules at all and one agency had previously completed a cost estimate but no longer had confidence in those calculations and therefore, planned to do a new cost-benefit analysis. OMB is sponsoring the development of a standardized cost model that could help agencies provide future estimates based on a common set of assumptions, estimates, and calculations.

Selected Agencies' Master Program Schedules Are Not Complete

The success of a program depends in part on having an integrated and reliable master schedule that defines when and how long work will occur and how one activity is related to another. A program schedule provides not only a road map for systematic project execution but also the means by which to gauge progress, identify and resolve potential problems, and promote accountability at all levels of the program. A schedule also provides a time sequence for the duration of a program's activities and furthers an understanding of both the dates for major milestones and the activities that drive the schedule. Our research has identified four select attributes of properly sequenced schedule activities that are essential for a reliable schedule network.[20] Table 6 provides a detailed description of these attributes.

Table 6: Select Attributes of Properly Sequenced Schedule Activities

Attribute	Definition
Identified dependencies	Activities that are related within a schedule network are referred to as predecessors and successors (i.e., dependencies). The purpose of a dependency is to depict the sequence of occurrence between activities. Except for the start and finish milestones, every activity within the schedule should have at least one predecessor and at least one successor. Identifying all interdependencies between activities is necessary for the schedule to properly calculate dates and predict changes in the future. Without the right linkages, activities that slip early in the schedule do not transmit delays to activities that should depend on them. When this happens, the schedule will not provide a sufficient basis for understanding the program as a whole, and users of the schedule will lack confidence in the dates and the critical path.
No dangling activities	Dangling activities have scheduling relationships that are not properly tied to an activity's start or end date. Each activity's start date—other than the start and finish milestones—must be driven by a predecessor activity, and each activity's finish date must drive a successor activity's start or finish. Dangling activities, a form of incomplete schedule logic, can interfere with the valid forecasting of scheduled activities.
No start-to-finish links	A relationship linking a predecessor and successor activity can take one of three forms: finish-to-start, start-to-start, and finish-to-finish. A fourth combination, the start-to-finish link, has the effect of directing a successor activity not to finish until its predecessor activity starts, in effect reversing the expected flow of effort. (For example, instead of creating an activity sequence in which a system is developed and then deployed, the start-to-finish link would require that deployment cannot be completed until system development has begun.) Its use is widely discouraged because it is counterintuitive and it overcomplicates the schedule network.
No summary links	Summary activities should not have relationships because their start and finish dates are derived from lower-level activities. Therefore, there is no need for relationships on a summary activity in a properly networked schedule.

Source: GAO.

Of the five agencies selected, three agencies (Agriculture, VA, and DHS) provided their consolidation master program schedules and two agencies (Interior and Transportation) did not provide a master program schedule that we could evaluate.[21] Of the three agencies that provided schedules, Agriculture and VA provided a single master schedule and DHS provided 4 schedules representing different aspects of the department's future

---

[20]GAO-12-120G.

[21]Interior provided a schedule, but not in time to be included in this evaluation. Similarly, Transportation officials told us that their FDCCI schedule was not in an electronic format that we could analyze and further, was only a task included in a much larger schedule for departmental IT projects.

consolidation plans. However, none of these agencies' schedules is fully compliant with the four attributes, although each agency was at least partially consistent with these practices. Table 7 provides an assessment of the agencies' consistency with the four attributes of properly sequenced schedule activities. A discussion of the analysis of each characteristic follows the table.

Table 7: Assessment of Consistency of Agencies' Schedules with Attributes of a Properly Sequenced Schedule

Attribute	Agriculture	DHS	VA
Identified dependencies	◑	◑	◑
No dangling activities	●	◑	●
No start-to-finish links	●	◑	●
No summary links	●	◑	○

Source: GAO analysis of agency data.

● – the schedule(s) addresses all aspects of this practice.

◑ – the schedule(s) addresses some, but not all, aspects of this practice.

○ – the schedule(s) addresses no aspects of this practice.

- **Identified dependencies.** None of the three agencies' schedules is fully consistent with this practice. Specifically, two of DHS's schedules have activities missing predecessors, successors, or both. Additionally, almost half of Agriculture's activities, and almost 40 percent of VA's, have a similar condition.

- **No dangling activities.** Two of the three agencies are consistent with this practice and one agency is partially consistent. For example, neither schedule for Agriculture or VA has any dangling activities. In contrast, two of DHS's four schedules do not have dangling activities, while the remaining two do have such activities.

- **No start-to-finish links.** Two of the three agencies' schedules are consistent with this practice and one agency's schedule is partially consistent. Both of Agriculture and VA's schedules are consistent with this practice and have no start-to-finish links. However, while three of DHS's schedules do not have start-to-finish links, one schedule does.

- **No summary links.** One of the three agencies was consistent with this practice, one agency was partially consistent, and one agency was not consistent. Specifically, Agriculture's schedule does not have any summary links, while only one of DHS's schedules meets the same condition. Three of DHS's schedules include summary links, as does VA's schedule.

Department officials gave a variety of reasons why their respective department did not provide documentation of a completed master program schedule:

- An Agriculture official told us that the department had a detailed schedule for every individual closure, but that because those projects are not necessarily linked to one another, there was no need to link these activities in a master schedule. However, leading practices demonstrate that even a summary master schedule should be a roll-up of lower-level schedules and reflect milestones that are automatically calculated through the established network logic between planned activities. A schedule with proper logic can predict impacts on the project's planned finish date of, among other things, misallocated resources, delayed activities, external events, scope changes, and unrealistic deadlines.

- DHS's consolidation program manager stated that the department provided separate schedules because schedules are developed for individual facilities when placed under contract for closure. However, leading practices show that a program schedule should include the entire required scope of effort, including the effort necessary from all government, contractors, and other key parties for a program's successful execution from start to finish. The DHS consolidation program manager acknowledged that the schedules in question were developed by contractors and that the department plans to incorporate the suggested best practices as appropriate.

- A VA official told us that because some of the tasks in the department's schedule are expected to start on particular dates to ensure funding is available for the project task, they do not have predecessor tasks. While this can be a permissible step when the schedule constraints are clearly identified, the VA official was able to provide some, but not all, of those constraints. The VA official further told us that unnecessary tasks and constraints have since been removed from the department's schedule.

- Interior officials stated that the department's master program schedule was not yet complete.

- Transportation's consolidation program manager stated that the department does not have a master program schedule dedicated to the FDCCI. Rather, the consolidation effort appears as a task on the department's master IT projects schedule.

In the absence of program schedules constructed in accordance with scheduling best practices, the agencies we evaluated are at risk of moving forward with their consolidation efforts despite having incomplete information that defines when and how long work will occur and how activities are related to each other.

Selected Agencies' Cost Estimates Are Not Reliable

We have reported that the ability to generate a reliable cost estimate, such as a cost-benefit analysis, is a critical function necessary to support OMB's capital programming process.[22] Such estimates should also include information on the benefits of the project. Without such estimates, agencies are at risk of experiencing cost overruns, missed deadlines, and performance shortfalls. Our research has identified a number of best practices that are the basis of effective program cost estimating and should result in reliable and valid cost estimates that management can use for making informed decisions. Table 8 provides a detailed description of the four characteristics of a high-quality and reliable cost estimate.

---

[22]GAO-09-3SP.

Table 8: Characteristics of a High-quality and Reliable Cost Estimate

Characteristic	Description
Comprehensive	The cost estimate should include all life cycle costs, completely define the program, reflect the current schedule, and be technically reasonable. The cost estimate work breakdown structure should be product-oriented, traceable to the statement of work/objective, and at an appropriate level of detail to ensure that cost elements are neither omitted nor double-counted. The estimate should document all cost-influencing ground rules and assumptions.
Well-documented	The estimate documentation should capture the source data used, the reliability of the data, and how the data were normalized and should describe in sufficient detail the calculations performed and the estimating methodology used to derive each element's cost. The documentation should describe step by step how the estimate was developed so that a cost analyst unfamiliar with the program could understand what was done and replicate it. The documentation should further discuss the technical baseline description and the data in the baseline should be consistent with the estimate, as well as provide evidence that the cost estimate was reviewed and accepted by management.
Accurate	The cost estimate results should be unbiased, not overly conservative or optimistic and based on an assessment of most likely costs and the estimate should be adjusted properly for inflation. The estimate should contain few, if any, minor mistakes and be regularly updated to reflect significant changes in the program so that it always reflects current status. Variances between planned and actual costs should be documented, explained, and reviewed and the estimate should be based on a historical record of cost estimating and actual experiences from other comparable programs.
Credible	The cost estimate should include a sensitivity analysis that identifies a range of possible costs based on varying major assumptions, parameters, and data inputs. A risk and uncertainty analysis should be conducted that quantifies the imperfectly understood risks and identifies the effects of changing key cost driver assumptions and factors. Major cost elements should be crossed-checked to see whether results were similar. An independent cost estimate should be conducted by a group outside the acquiring organization to determine whether other estimating methods produce similar results.

Source: GAO.

Of the five agencies selected, four (Agriculture, DHS, Interior, and VA) provided supporting documentation used to calculate the cost estimates found in the agencies' consolidation plans and one (Transportation) did not. Transportation officials explained that they were no longer confident in their prior estimates and they planned to undertake a new cost-benefit analysis in 2012. None of the four agencies' estimates was fully compliant with best practices, although all of the estimates were at least minimally consistent with these practices. Table 9 provides an assessment of the estimates' consistency with the characteristics of a reliable cost estimate. A discussion of the analysis of each characteristic follows the table.

Table 9: Assessment of Consistency of Agencies' Cost Estimates with Best Practices

Characteristic	Agriculture	DHS	Interior	VA
Comprehensive	◑	◑	◑	◑
Well-documented	◔	◔	◑	◕
Accurate	◔	◔	◔	◔
Credible	◔	◔	◑	◔

Source: GAO analysis of agency data.

● – the agency provides complete evidence that satisfies the entire criterion.

◕ – the agency provides evidence that satisfies most of the criterion.

◑ – the agency provides evidence that satisfies about half of the criterion.

◔ – the agency provides evidence that satisfies a few of the criterion.

○ – the agency provides no evidence that satisfies any of the criterion.

- **Comprehensive.** None of the estimates are fully consistent with this practice, although all four estimates satisfy about half of the criterion for this practice. For example, Agriculture includes most related costs and estimate assumptions, but does not include a work breakdown structure. Similarly, Interior includes most related costs and estimate assumptions, but also does not include a work breakdown structure.

- **Well-documented.** None of the estimates fully satisfy this practice. Specifically, one estimate satisfies most, but not all, of the practice, one estimate satisfies about half of the criterion for the practice, and two estimates satisfy a few of the criterion for the practice. For example, Interior documents its technical baseline but does not fully document how the estimate was developed. VA describes how its calculations were performed and discusses the estimate's technical baseline, but satisfied only half of the criteria describing how the estimate was performed.

- **Accurate.** None of the estimates fully satisfied this practice. One estimate satisfied about half of the practice and three estimates satisfied some of the practice. For example, Agriculture's estimate is partially based on historical estimates, but has not been updated since March 2009. Additionally, while DHS updated its estimate in July 2011, it did not adjust for inflation or document variations between planned and actual costs.

- **Credible.** None of the estimates fully satisfied this practice. One estimate satisfied about half the practice and three estimates satisfied some of the practice. For example, DHS addressed some aspects of a risk and uncertainty analysis, but did not conduct an estimate sensitivity analysis. Conversely, VA addressed some aspects of an estimate sensitivity analysis, but did not conduct a risk and uncertainty analysis. Neither agency conducted an independent cost estimate.

Agency officials gave a variety of reasons for why their cost estimates were not complete. For example, the Agriculture CIO indicated that the department's estimate was performed several years ago by a contractor and additional documentation was difficult to acquire. Additionally, Interior's consolidation program manager stated that the department was in the process of revising its cost estimate using OMB's cost model, but the effort was not yet complete. Further, Interior's consolidation plan describes several efforts to estimate costs that the department ultimately did not include in their plan and indicates that the department will address this in a future deliverable. In May 2012, Interior officials stated that they recently provided this information to OMB. VA officials stated that they did not provide previous cost estimate documentation because the department expected to revise its cost estimate using new information regarding cost assumptions and that this information would affect life-cycle cost estimates. The DHS consolidation program manager noted that the department is now taking a different approach towards cost estimates through the use of enterprisewide contracts. Regarding Transportation, although it reported FDCCI-related estimated savings of over $26 million in its 2010 plan, the department's updated consolidation plan states that the original cost estimates were no longer relevant and the department is in the process of conducting a new estimating effort that was not completed in time for the plan's submission. Further, in March 2012, a department official confirmed that Transportation no longer felt comfortable with the original savings estimate and that planned cost savings were being reevaluated. The official further stated the department intends to complete a new cost-benefit analysis.

Between the five agencies that we reviewed, there are plans to consolidate 375 data centers of all sizes. In the absence of reliable cost estimates, these five agencies are exposed to the types of risks that we have reported to be recurring problems in our program reviews—namely cost overruns, missed deadlines, and performance shortfalls. Because of the importance of a high-quality cost estimate to consolidation efforts as significant as these, it will be important for these agencies to work to improve their cost estimates, thus providing information on which management can make well-informed decisions as the agencies move towards their 2015 targets.

OMB Developed a Model to Help Agencies Plan Consolidations, but Does Not Require Its Use

To assist agencies in their data center consolidation efforts, the FDCCI Data Center Consolidation Task Force developed a standard Total Cost of Ownership (TCO) model in order to provide a comprehensive tool to help to inform consolidation decision making, model consolidation paths, and assist with the development of cost savings figures and funding needs. OMB provided the model to agencies for voluntary use starting in January 2012, noting that it is intended to provide a uniform and consistent method to derive agency cost savings figures and a modeling and simulation tool to inform consolidation decisions.

At a high level, agencies load their raw agency inventory data into the spreadsheet-based model to develop three outputs:

- an "as is" view of current costs;

- a 5-year projection of costs based on maintaining current equipment and facilities at current growth rates; and

- a 5-year projection of costs, including equipment and facilities counts, based on the agency's planned data center closure and efficiency targets.

The model relies on a number of built-in assumptions—based on best practices in the public and private sectors and grouped into categories such as facilities, hardware, and software—to provide its outputs. The model also recognizes some limitations, such as an inability to capture costing data for individual facilities and an inability to recognize individual costs for hardware and software. To compensate, the model applies universal values for such information, while recognizing the inaccuracies this may cause in some costing elements. The model further allows agencies to adjust specific variables to input costs that are atypical or not already anticipated by the model. According to an official from the GSA program management office that maintains the cost model, while not intended to capture comprehensive program costs, the model does provide agencies with the ability to customize the input information to make it as comprehensive as they need it to be. As a result, agencies could use this tool to provide more consistent and reliable cost estimates. Moreover, the model provides standardized cost calculations, adjustment for inflation, and a scenario-analysis tool that agencies can use to analyze alternatives and develop plans. Thus, it can be used as a tool to help agencies improve their consolidation planning.

Officials from several agencies told us that they plan to use the TCO model in future cost estimating efforts. For example, a Transportation official told us that the department intends to use the model as it recalculates its cost-benefit estimate. Additionally, the Interior consolidation program manager stated that the department planned to use the model to determine power estimates. Officials from other agencies, such as SSA and EPA, told us that the model was being considered for future use.

Use of the TCO model could provide more consistent and reliable cost estimates, but using the model is currently voluntary. In light of the limitations identified above in our review of the five agencies' cost estimates, the deployment of a standardized tool for planning consolidation efforts could help ensure that agencies develop consistent and uniform projections. Until OMB requires agencies to use the model, agencies will likely continue to use a variety of methodologies and assumptions in establishing consolidation estimates, and it will remain difficult to summarize projections across agencies.

Agencies Have Experienced Consolidation Successes and Continue to Report Challenges

Agencies reported experiencing multiple areas of success in their consolidation efforts. Specifically, 20 agencies identified 34 areas of success, with the number of agencies reporting a particular success ranging from 9 to 1. However, only 3 successes were identified by multiple agencies and, of those, 2 represent over 45 percent of the total reported successes. Four agencies—Justice, Transportation, NSF, and SSA—did not report any successes. Table 10 details the reported successes as well as the number of agencies identifying that area of success; the two most common areas are further discussed after the table.

Table 10: Agency Consolidation Successes

Reported areas of success	Number of agencies
Focusing on virtualization and cloud services as consolidation solutions	9
Working with other agencies and components to find consolidation opportunities	8
Ensuring a more comprehensive asset inventory	2
Overcoming internal politics	1
Developing and using a "mobile data center" to migrate hardware and facilitate data transfer	1
Implementing new services to expedite consolidation projects	1
Transitioning end-user support to a hosting agency, enabling site closure	1
Developing standardized templates for consolidation plan elements	1
Consolidating multiple e-mail systems into one cloud-based provider	1
Using Energy Performance Contracting to rehabilitate buildings	1
Developing a profiling tool to allow local managers to directly enter inventory information	1
Realizing savings and efficiencies from the migration to new enterprise data centers	1
Increasing implementation of "as a service" offerings to reduce overall costs of operations	1
Improving service levels	1
Improving knowledge management	1
Using the Data Center Consolidation Task Force as a forum for discussing challenges and identifying potential synergies between agencies	1
Negotiating carefully with vendors	1
Implementing shared services	1

Source: GAO analysis of agency data and interviews with agency officials.

Agencies Report That Virtualization and Cloud Services Have Produced Cost Savings

Virtualization is a technology that allows multiple, software-based machines with different operating systems, to run in isolation, side-by-side, on the same physical machine. Cloud computing is an emerging form of computing that relies on Internet-based services and resources to provide computing services to customers, while freeing them from the burden and costs of maintaining the underlying infrastructure. OMB suggests both technologies as agency approaches, along with decommissioning and consolidation. Nine agencies reported that focusing on virtualization and cloud computing have proven successful for their consolidation efforts.

GAO-12-742 Data Center Consolidation

The Interior consolidation program manager cited virtualization as the department's greatest consolidation success, noting the efforts of the department's Bureau of Indian Affairs as an example. Specifically, Interior has documented virtualization as a key enabler in the efforts of the bureau to close data centers. After closing 11 data centers in fiscal year 2011, the bureau turned its attention to remote sites with more than three servers. Through virtualization, the bureau was able to reduce all remote sites to either one or two physical servers. Additionally, on a site-by-site basis, other application and database servers were either virtualized or migrated to one of two primary bureau data centers. In doing so, the bureau's virtualization effort reportedly produced over $114,000 in cost avoidance savings for fiscal year 2011, is expected to produce over $66,000 in savings for fiscal year 2012, and is planned to produce further savings of $66,000 annually. Table 11 details reductions and savings that the bureau has already realized and plans for the future.

Table 11: Reported Savings from Bureau of Indian Affairs Virtualization

Category	4th quarter 2010	4th quarter 2011	4th quarter 2012 (planned)
Total data centers	14	3	1
Percent change from 2010 data centers	—	-82.35%	-88.23%
Total data center servers	367	460	71
Percent change from 2010 server count	—	+25.34%	-80.65%
Aggregate data center energy usage (kWh/year)	1,405,454	1,199,682	127,020
Percent change from 2010 energy usage	—	-14.64%	-90.96%
Aggregate data center energy costs per year	$101,192	$86,377	$9,145
Energy cost reduction	—	$14,815	$77,231
Cost savings of virtualization	—	$114,240	$66,261

Source: Department of the Interior.

Other agencies also reported virtualization as a key factor in being able to realize resource reductions. For example, EPA officials told us that the agency was using virtualization to optimize their IT infrastructure. In 2011, the agency virtualized over 360 servers, increasing the agency's virtualization by 6 percent. In 2012, the agency plans to consolidate and virtualize email hosting services, allowing the agency to decommission 14 percent (or over 300) of its physical servers, and migrate the agency's email gateways to cloud services. In one EPA facility, the agency will migrate over 100 servers from eight server rooms to one primary data center. Additionally, NRC reports that it used virtualization to exceed its 2011 goals for Windows server reductions. Specifically, the agency was able to exceed its goal of reducing 13 servers and actually reduced 33 physical servers, a reduction of more than 10 percent from its baseline of 288 servers. Further, OPM officials reported that within 15 months, the agency was able to increase the virtualization of its Windows servers from 15 percent to 50 percent, resulting in cost savings for the agency.

Other agencies reported on the less tangible, but still significant, importance of virtualization to their efforts. An Education official told us that the department's biggest success has come from focusing on virtualization, rather than physical consolidation. DHS reported that the increased implementation of virtualization will reduce the overall costs of the department's migration and postmigration operations. Further, officials from Labor told us that they expect virtualization to have an impact on the results of their consolidation, but that they had not yet documented any of those results.

Officials from three agencies also shared with us the advantages of moving their organizations to cloud services. Specifically, a DHS official told us that the department's cloud services technology was becoming operational and as a result, costs savings were becoming evident versus traditional consolidation. Whereas 2 years ago, the department had nothing in the cloud, a large percentage of services were now moving in that direction. The official specifically noted a DHS component that was originally only going to move to its own physical infrastructure, but was now joining with other components because of the benefits of moving services to the cloud. A HUD official stated that the department's successes were related to higher efficiency and utilization of computing and storage resources. Essentially, HUD embarked on a cloud-like solution—by means of the department's existing outsourcing contract—before cloud computing really existed as a service. As a result, the official noted that the department has been receiving a number of benefits such as green IT, regular technology refreshes, and high utilization of resources. A second HUD official noted that the department has been rated across the government as having the third-highest computing utilization and the second-most efficient use of storage capacity. Further, and as mentioned earlier, an EPA official noted that the migration of EPA's email gateways to cloud services will enable the agency to decommission 14 percent (over 300) of the agency's physical servers.

Agencies and Components Are Working Together to Identify Consolidation Opportunities

Eight agencies reported consolidation successes that had been realized through agencies working together, both within and outside of their department, to identify consolidation opportunities. For example, several of the agencies that reported success with virtualization, as discussed earlier, also reported working with other departmental components as a key enabler of resulting savings. Specifically, Interior reported that as part of the department's closing of 11 Bureau of Indian Affairs data centers in fiscal year 2011, two facilities were consolidated with other Interior bureaus, resulting in a reduction of 43 of the bureau's 65 servers and producing immediate cost avoidance savings of over $114,000. Defense noted the willingness of its components to adopt the departmental strategy of first looking to the Defense Information Systems Agency for application and data hosting before pursuing any other options. Further, a SBA official told us that one success from the consolidation effort was that agencies have been looking for ways to work together. Specifically, the official cited the SBA's effort to reach out to another agency in order to craft an interagency agreement to work together and move part of their operations into the hosting agency's systems. A second agency official noted that because of this, the hosting agency has contacted SBA to make sure that it included SBA's needs in its planning and requests. Additionally, a DHS official told us that departmental components were joining together to move services to the cloud.

There were also reported successes in working with external agencies. For example, VA reported that the department was successful in working with the Defense Information Systems Agency on an agreement to consolidate mission critical enterprise IT systems into the agency's Defense Enterprise Computing Centers. The department noted that considerable cost savings could be realized by entering into such an interagency agreement, as opposed to leasing from a commercial site, for mission critical health record systems. Additionally, a HHS official similarly reported that the department's Indian Health Service, which has small data centers that cannot close because of communication difficulties in their locations, recognized that Interior's Bureau of Indian Affairs had a data center in close proximity to an Indian Health Service facility. Consequently, the service was able to share space with the bureau and consolidate one of its data centers and the service is now looking for similar opportunities that will allow HHS to consolidate further. Further, Labor officials told us that the department was consolidating small server rooms in regional offices to co-located facilities and that this approach was expected to reduce costs.

The consolidation successes experienced by agencies indicate that aspects of FDCCI are moving forward as planned. Further, almost half of these reported accomplishments directly relate to key tenets of OMB's plans for the initiative, demonstrating that OMB has developed a consolidation road map that provides realistic means by which agencies can achieve their goals.

Agencies Continue to Report Consolidation Challenges, but the Types of Challenges Are Evolving

In 2011, we reported on the challenges that agencies were facing during data center consolidations. These included challenges related to FDCCI as well as those that were cultural, funding related, operational, and technical. In 2012, agencies have continued to report many of the same challenges, have reported new challenges, and have stopped reporting challenges they previously identified. As we found in 2011, some challenges are more common than others. Specifically, the number of agencies reporting a particular challenge range from 15 to 1. Additionally, 25 challenges reported in 2011 were not reported in 2012. Two agencies, HUD and NSF, did not report any challenges. Table 12 details the reported challenges, the numbers of agencies experiencing that challenge, and identifies the challenges no longer being reported by agencies. The table is followed by a discussion of the most prevalent challenges.

Table 12: Challenges Encountered by Agencies in 2011 and 2012, Including Those No Longer Reported

		Number of agencies reporting	
Challenge type	Challenge	2011	2012
Initiative-related (33)	Obtaining power usage information, as required by OMB	19	15
	Providing good quality asset inventories, as required by OMB	4	10
	Adjusting as OMB modified its definition of "data center"	2	5
	Aligning data center consolidation with other initiatives	4	1
	Political interest in FDCCI consolidation target facilities	0	1
	Confusing or conflicting metrics specified in OMB templates	0	1
	Identifying and quantifying actual costs associated with data center facilities and operational support	0	1
	Meeting tight planning deadlines for OMB's milestones	11	0
	Including consolidation information in middle of fiscal year 2012 budget cycle	4	0
	Working towards an undefined future state of the data center consolidation initiative	1	0
	Reporting savings in an already consolidated organization	1	0
	Applying same FDCCI targets to all agencies, regardless of situation	1	0
Cultural (12)	Accepting cultural change that is part of consolidation	15	5
	Obtaining enterprise buy-in to the consolidation effort	1	5
	Implementing FDCCI in an organizational structure, such as a decentralized enterprise, that is not geared towards consolidation	8	2

GAO-12-742 Data Center Consolidation

Challenge type	Challenge	Number of agencies reporting	
		2011	2012
	Assuming significant new responsibilities as a result of consolidation	2	0
Funding (11)	Acquiring funding required for consolidation and migration efforts	11	9
	Identifying cost savings to be realized by consolidation	9	2
	Reimbursing external organizations for shared services/multi-tenancy	2	0
	Projecting cost information	1	0
	Accounting for costs in a flat fee lease	1	0
	Planning consolidation efforts across components with differing funding streams	1	0
Operational (11)	Difficulty with procurement process	0	3
	Technology and resource constraints	0	2
	Implementing cloud computing	3	1
	Relocating displaced staff	1	1
	Implementing shared services	0	1
	Implementing virtualization	0	1
	No motivation for IT organizations to reduce IT system energy costs when they do not pay for power costs	0	1
	Environmental challenges	0	1
	Maintaining services during consolidation transition	9	0
	Managing physical infrastructure	2	0
	Creating appropriate service-level agreements with other organizations	2	0
	Locating a suitable site for data center	2	0
	Transitioning to a new service provider	1	0
	Understanding the limitations of facilities	1	0
Technical (7)	Planning migration strategy	2	7
	Maintaining appropriate level of system security	3	0
	Configuring the network for consolidation	2	0
	Forecasting capacity and seasonal demand	2	0
	Meshing data from multiple locations	2	0
	Ensuring enough bandwidth for the network	2	0
	Creating shared standards (including system and physical security, storage, and risk management) for co-located resources and services	1	0
	Testing of changed applications	1	0
	Overseeing a vendor's security; certification and accreditation are set up and performed	1	0
	Analyzing business needs and solutions to be sure of a good fit	1	0

Source: GAO analysis of agency data and interviews with agency officials.

Initiative-related Challenges	Agencies reported seven challenges that are specific to FDCCI, including obtaining power usage and providing good quality asset inventories, both as required by OMB. Specifically, 15 agencies reported that obtaining power usage information was a challenge, which is less than the 19 agencies that reported this challenge last year. For example, a NASA official told us that the agency only had one data center (out of 79) that was fully metered, but that the agency was working to establish metering capabilities at several more locations. An SBA official told us that the agency was still working to complete a power audit, but that it was questionable whether such an audit would be worth the amount of work required to install separate power meters in leased facilities. A USAID official reported that none of the agency's facilities were metered and that the agency was not a landlord for any of its facilities, making power information difficult to obtain. Further, 10 agencies reported that providing good quality inventories was a challenge, which is more than the 4 agencies that reported this challenge last year. For example, an EPA official told us that the agency had trouble determining cost information for its server rooms because most were facilities within office spaces and which were part of larger federal leases or within GSA buildings. As a result, EPA focused their efforts on facilities greater than 500 square feet. Additionally, a Defense official reported that that gathering and verifying inventory information for an organization the size of the department was challenging.
Cultural Challenges	Agencies reported three cultural challenges to data center consolidation, including accepting cultural change that is part of consolidation and obtaining enterprise buy-in to the consolidation effort. One of the most prevalently reported cultural challenges, accepting cultural change, was cited by 5 agencies, which is 10 fewer agencies than last year. For example, Energy found that there was a perceived need for each facility or departmental organization to have "ownership" of their own data centers and server rooms in order to support their business or mission needs. Justice recognized that moving from the department's current environment to a more unified, standardized, and cost-efficient approach for providing data center services requires change and consequently, efforts were underway to drive more significant consolidation. Another commonly reported cultural challenge was obtaining enterprise buy-in to the consolidation effort, which was reported by 5 agencies—an increase from the single agency that reported this last year. For example, DHS reported their consolidation effort to be a multistakeholder operation that required immense amounts of coordination and found that delays and issues arose when various stakeholders maintained differing visions, expectations, and commitment to the effort. Further, NRC reported that

one of its main challenges was managing the level of coordination required by the number of internal and external entities involved in planning and the related activities that need to happen simultaneously.

Funding Challenges

Agencies reported two funding challenges: acquiring the funding needed for consolidation and identifying cost savings to be realized by consolidation. Nine agencies reported challenges with acquiring funding, which is slightly fewer than the 11 agencies that reported this challenge last year. For example, Energy reported that the department had little or no funding available to invest in data center measurement systems, server utilizations assessments, or consolidation projects. Additionally, both Justice and Transportation reported challenges in providing upfront funding for consolidation efforts before cost savings accrue. Two agencies reported challenges with identifying cost savings, a decrease from the 9 agencies that reported this challenge last year. For example, an Interior official noted that the department would likely not be able to report on savings for 2011 because most bureaus absorbed the cost of consolidation within their budgets. Although site-specific plans were required by the department, most did not address costs. Additionally, an SSA official noted that the agency currently had too many uncertainties surrounding its consolidation effort to perform a cost-benefit analysis.

Operational Challenges

Agencies reported eight operational challenges, including difficulties with procurement and technology and resource constraints, neither of which had been reported in 2011. Three agencies encountered challenges with procurement, including DHS, which had to create a team to streamline projects through the department's procurement process. GSA reported encountering construction contracting challenges on all three of the agency's calendar year 2011 data center consolidations. These contract challenges included: vendors that could not meet award schedules, nonresponsive vendors, and long lead times for some IT equipment. To counter such delays, GSA increased the time allotted for planned contracting efforts and vendor delivery schedules. Additionally, two agencies reported challenges with technology and resource constraints. Specifically, EPA reported encountering minor delays in consolidation plan execution due to such constraints and NRC reported another of its main challenges to consolidation being available resources and the impact on its critical path to consolidation, which is the timely completion of the agency's new headquarters building.

Technical Challenges

Agencies reported only one technical challenge to consolidation, planning a migration strategy. Specifically, this was reported by seven agencies, an increase from the two agencies that reported this in 2011. For example, Transportation's consolidation plan notes that in the department's organization, it is a long process to identify possible consolidations, present them to management, then to users, and then work the technical side of migrations. Transportation's plan also noted that application mapping is a very difficult and time-consuming activity, but cannot be skipped in a successful completion of a migration. Further, an Education official told us that the department had to develop a two-step approach for migrating files after encountering technical issues with an earlier migration effort. Finally, Commerce reported in its consolidation plan that detailed consolidation planning was critical due to the number of moving parts and potential impact on applications and customers.

As we have previously reported, one approach agencies can use to manage challenges such as the ones described above is through risk management processes. In 2011, we reported that less than half of the agencies included a discussion of risk management in their data center consolidation plans. As we stated earlier, 18 of the agencies, or 75 percent, now fully address risk management. By addressing consolidation risk, agencies have better positioned themselves to manage the challenges they have identified.

In any significant IT initiative, it is important that both successes and challenges be highlighted. In the case of FDCCI, a success highlights approaches and strategies that are helping agencies to meet their consolidation targets and fulfill the intent of the initiative. Conversely, a challenge identifies an area where agencies are struggling to meet the requirements and intent of this governmentwide effort. The two most reported consolidation successes are both key tenets of OMB's FDCCI: the use of virtualization and cloud services, and working with other agencies to find consolidation opportunities. Alternately, the three most reported challenges directly impact the ability of FDCCI to meet its goals: gathering power usage information, developing good quality data center inventories, and acquiring the funding needed for consolidation. In light of how closely the successes and challenges reported by agencies relate to FDCCI, it will be important for OMB to continue to provide leadership and guidance to the initiative. This includes, as we have previously recommended, utilizing the existing accountability infrastructure of the Data Center Consolidation Task Force to assess agency consolidation plans to ensure they are complete and to monitor the agencies' implementation of their plans.[23]

Conclusions

With agencies reporting having closed 286 data centers by the end of 2011 and planning to close an additional 346 centers by the end of 2012, the data center consolidation initiative is expected to realize about $2.4 billion in cost savings through 2015. OMB now requires agencies to annually update both their data center inventories and their consolidation plans and has expanded the required content of both. However, agencies' consolidation and savings goals continue to be built on incomplete inventories and plans. To better ensure that FDCCI improves governmental efficiency and achieves promised cost savings, we are reiterating our prior recommendation to the department secretaries and agency heads of the 24 departments and agencies participating in the federal data center consolidation initiative to fully complete their consolidation inventories and plans expeditiously.[24]

As OMB refines its approach to the data center consolidation initiative, it provides updated guidance to agencies. However, three agencies did not learn of the most recent changes in OMB's required formats, in part because the guidance was provided in meetings and not in a formal letter from the Federal CIO to agency CIOs or disseminated on the website where all prior guidance had been disseminated. Until OMB uses more structured mechanisms to disseminate its guidance, it runs the risk that agencies will not learn of important changes in format or approach.

Additionally, basic consolidation plan requirements, such as the need for schedules and cost estimates, are still unmet by almost 70 percent of the agencies. Among the five agencies selected for a detailed review, none of the agencies' master schedules and estimates were completed in a manner consistent with best practices. For example, none of the agencies was able to demonstrate that its cost estimates were accurate, credible, or comprehensive. OMB's cost of ownership model should help address a number of planning concerns. As more agencies use the model, OMB can use the model to ensure consistent planning and reporting on consolidation efforts across FDCCI. However, agencies' use of the model

[23]GAO-11-565.

[24]GAO-11-565.

is still voluntary. Until OMB requires agencies to use the model, it may miss opportunities to ensure consistency among agencies and it will remain difficult to summarize projections across agencies.

As the federal consolidation effort matures, agencies are beginning to realize successes. These constructive experiences, which stem from OMB's recommended consolidation strategies, indicate that FDCCI is moving in the right direction. However, as agencies work towards their consolidation goals, many continue to report challenges related to gathering the necessary technical information and funding the consolidation itself. While these challenges are consistent with those reported in the past, over 25 previous challenges were no longer reported by the agencies. Such a dynamic environment reinforces the need for agencies to remain in communication in order to facilitate knowledge sharing and transfer and for OMB to continue to provide leadership and guidance.

Recommendations for Executive Action

In addition to reiterating our prior recommendation to agencies to complete the missing elements of their inventories and plans, we are making two recommendations to OMB. Specifically, we recommend that the Director of OMB direct the Federal CIO to

- ensure that all future revisions to the guidance on data center consolidation inventories and plans are defined in OMB memorandum and posted to the FDCCI public website in a manner consistent with the guidance published in 2010, and

- ensure agencies utilize OMB's Total Cost of Ownership model as a standardized planning tool across the consolidation initiative.

In addition, we recommend that the Secretaries of Agriculture, Homeland Security, Interior, Transportation, and Veterans Affairs direct their component agencies and their data center consolidation program managers to implement recognized best practices when completing required program schedules and cost-benefit analyses.

Agency Comments and Our Evaluation

We received comments on a draft of our report from OMB, the 5 agencies to which we made recommendations, and the other 19 agencies mentioned in the report. Specifically, OMB and the 5 agencies to which we made recommendations either agreed with, or had no comment on, the recommendations and the other 19 agencies had no specific comments on our recommendations. Multiple agencies also provided technical comments, which we incorporated as appropriate. Each agency's comments are discussed in more detail below.

- In oral comments, OMB officials, including the Deputy Federal CIO and staff from the Office of E-government and Information Technology and the Office of the General Counsel, stated that they generally agreed with, and described planned actions to implement, our recommendations. These officials also provided technical comments, which we have incorporated as appropriate.

- In written comments, Agriculture's Acting CIO stated that the department concurred with the content of the report and had no comments. The department offered no comments on our recommendations. The department also provided technical comments, which we have incorporated as appropriate. Agriculture's written comments are provided in appendix III.

- In written comments, DHS's Director of the Departmental GAO/OIG Liaison Office concurred with our recommendation, commented on the current and planned state of the department's consolidation efforts, and outlined actions the department plans to take to implement our recommendation and update its data center inventory and consolidation plan. The department also provided technical comments, which we have incorporated as appropriate. DHS's written comments are provided in appendix IV.

- In written comments, Interior's Assistant Secretary for Policy, Management and Budget stated the department concurred with the report's finding and recommendations, commented on the current status of the department's consolidation efforts, and described the department's plans to develop savings and cost avoidance projections. The department also provided technical comments, which we have incorporated as appropriate. Interior's written comments are provided in appendix V.

- In comments provided via e-mail, Transportation's Deputy Director of Audit Relations wrote that the department had no comments on the draft. The department offered no comments on the recommendations.

- In written comments, VA's Chief of Staff stated that the department generally agreed with our conclusions, concurred with our recommendation, and described planned actions to address our recommendation. The department also provided technical comments, which we have incorporated as appropriate. VA's written comments are provided in appendix VI.

- In written comments, Commerce's Acting Secretary concurred with the report's general findings as they applied to the department and with the specific reporting on the department's consolidation plan. Commerce's written comments are provided in appendix VII.

- In comments provided via e-mail, an audit liaison from Defense's Office of the CIO wrote that the department had no comments on the report.

- In comments provided via e-mail, an official from Education's Office of the Secretary wrote that the department had no comments on the report.

- In written comments, the Director of Energy's Corporate IT Project Management Office stated that the department concurred with the findings reported for Energy and noted steps being taken by the department to address a consolidation challenge discussed in our report. The department also elaborated on facilities that we cited as not having been reported in Energy's FDCCI inventory. Energy's written comments are provided in appendix VIII.

- In written comments, HHS' Assistant Secretary for Legislation stated our report was an accurate representation of the department's 2011 data center inventory and consolidation plan and outlined actions the department plans to take to complete missing inventory and plan elements. HHS' written comments are provided in appendix IX.

- In comments provided via e-mail, a HUD audit liaison wrote that the department had no comments or concerns regarding the report.

- In comments provided via e-mail, an official from Justice's Office of the CIO wrote that the department had no comments on the report.

- In written comments, Labor's Assistant Secretary for Administration and Management stated that the department did not have any comments on the draft to contribute. Labor's written comments are provided in appendix X.

GAO-12-742 Data Center Consolidation

- In comments provided via e-mail, an official from State's Office of the Chief Financial Officer wrote that the department had no comments on the report.

- In comments provided via e-mail, Treasury's Deputy Assistant Secretary for Information Systems agreed with our report. The department also provided technical comments, which we have incorporated as appropriate.

- In written comments, the Director of EPA's Office of Technology Operation and Planning provided technical comments, which we have incorporated as appropriate. The agency did not comment on the report's findings.

- In comments provided via e-mail, an official from GSA's GAO/IG Audit Response Division wrote that the agency had no comments on the report.

- In comments provided via e-mail, the team lead for NASA's GAO/OIG Audit Liaison wrote that the agency was providing no comments on the report.

- In written comments, NSF's CIO stated that the agency generally agreed with our characterization of their consolidation plan, but disagreed with our assessment of the agency's master program schedule. The CIO asserted that we were provided with such a schedule, while also acknowledging that the schedule was inherently less detailed than those of agencies and departments with multiple components, but that it identified all NSF consolidation activities in the format and level of detail prescribed by OMB. However, OMB's guidance on master program schedules states that such schedules are to be created from the detailed implementation schedules provided by data center managers, as well as driven by related federal government activities, such as OMB reporting and budgeting. While we acknowledge that NSF's consolidation scope is less than that of some agencies, the high-level timeline presented as a master program schedule consists only of a single line item that states the fiscal year when NSF's data center will be decommissioned. Further, this timeline does not include any of the detailed implementation activities or key baseline milestones required by OMB. As such, we believe our evaluation is reasonable and appropriate. NSF's written comments are provided in appendix XI.

- In comments provided via e-mail, the NRC OIG and GAO Liaison wrote that the agency had reviewed the report and had no comments. The liaison also provided an update on NRC's plans to move to a single data center.

- In comments provided via e-mail, an official from OPM's Office of Internal Oversight and Compliance wrote that the agency had no comments on the report.

- In comments provided via e-mail, the program manager for SBA's Office of Congressional and Legislative Affairs provided technical comments, which we have incorporated as appropriate.

- In comments provided via e-mail, a SSA audit liaison wrote that the agency had no comments on the report.

- In comments provided via e-mail, an official from USAID's Office of the Chief Financial Officer wrote that the agency had no comments on the report.

We are sending copies of this report to interested congressional committees; the secretaries and agency heads of the departments and agencies addressed in this report; and other interested parties. In addition, the report will be available at no charge on GAO's website at http://www.gao.gov.

If you or your staffs have any questions on the matters discussed in this report, please contact me at (202) 512-9286 or pownerd@gao.gov. Contact points for our Offices of Congressional Relations and Public Affairs may be found on the last page of this report. GAO staff who made major contributions to this report are listed in appendix XII.

David A. Powner
Director
Information Technology
  Management Issues

The Honorable Joseph I. Lieberman
Chairman
The Honorable Susan M. Collins
Ranking Member
Committee on Homeland Security and Governmental Affairs
United States Senate

The Honorable Thomas R. Carper
Chairman
The Honorable Scott P. Brown
Ranking Member
Subcommittee on Federal Financial Management, Government
     Information, Federal Services, and International Security
Committee on Homeland Security and Governmental Affairs
United States Senate

The Honorable Darrell E. Issa
Chairman
The Honorable Elijah E. Cummings
Ranking Member
Committee on Oversight and Government Reform
House of Representatives

The Honorable James Lankford
Chairman
The Honorable Gerald E. Connolly
Ranking Member
Subcommittee on Technology, Information Policy,
     Intergovernmental Relations, and Procurement Reform
Committee on Oversight and Government Reform
House of Representatives

The Honorable Benjamin E. Quayle
House of Representatives

Appendix I: Objectives, Scope, and Methodology

Our objectives were to (1) evaluate the extent to which agencies have updated and verified their data center inventories and data center consolidation plans, (2) evaluate the extent to which selected agencies have adequately completed key elements of their consolidation plans, and (3) identify agencies' notable consolidation successes and challenges.

For this governmentwide review, we assessed the 24 departments and agencies (agencies) that were identified by the Office of Management and Budget (OMB) and the Federal Chief Information Officer (CIO) to be included in the Federal Data Center Consolidation Initiative (FDCCI). Table 13 lists these agencies.

Table 13: Chief Information Officers Council Departments and Agencies Participating in FDCCI

Departments	Agencies
Agriculture	Environmental Protection Agency
Commerce	General Services Administration
Defense	National Aeronautics and Space Administration
Education	National Science Foundation
Energy	Nuclear Regulatory Commission
Health and Human Services	Office of Personnel Management
Homeland Security	Small Business Administration
Housing and Urban Development	Social Security Administration
Interior	U.S. Agency for International Development
Justice	
Labor	
State	
Transportation	
Treasury	
Veterans Affairs	

Source: GAO analysis of OMB data.

To evaluate the agencies' updated data center inventories and consolidation plans, we reviewed OMB's guidance and identified key required elements for each type of document. We compared agency consolidation inventories and plans to OMB's required elements, and identified gaps and missing elements. We rated each element as "Yes" if the agency provides complete information; "Partial" if the agency provides some, but not all, of the information; and "No" if the agency does not

GAO-12-742 Data Center Consolidation

provide the information. We followed up with agencies to clarify our initial findings and to determine why parts of the inventories and plans were incomplete or missing, as applicable. We also compared our findings with those reported in 2011.[1] To assess the reliability of the data agencies provided in their data center inventories and plans, we reviewed the letters agencies were required to submit attesting to the completeness and reliability of their inventories and plans, we interviewed agency officials about the actions taken to verify their data, and reviewed those results against our past reviews of agency inventories and plans. We concluded that the data were sufficiently reliable for our purposes, which was to report on the completeness of the inventories and plans.

To evaluate the completion of key elements of selected agencies' consolidation plans, we selected two required plan elements, a master program schedule and a cost-benefit analysis, which is a type of cost estimate. In 2011, we reported that these two elements had the lowest reported completion rates among the FDCCI agencies.[2] We then selected five agencies that we reported in 2011 as having one or both of the two key elements. Specifically, the Departments of Agriculture (Agriculture), Homeland Security (DHS), and Interior (Interior) were the only agencies that reported having a completed master program schedule in our 2011 report. Similarly, DHS and the Departments of Transportation (Transportation) and Veterans Affairs (VA) were the three agencies that reported having a completed cost-benefit analysis in our 2011 report and that reported the greatest amount of anticipated savings. To assess the agencies' schedules, we compared copies of their consolidation master program schedules with relevant best practices compiled in a GAO exposure report issued in May 2012.[3] These practices include four select characteristics of properly sequenced schedule activities that are essential for a reliable schedule network, such as identifying all schedule dependencies and ensuring that all activities have proper relationships with each other. In conducting this analysis, for each schedule, we rated

---

[1]GAO, *Data Center Consolidation: Agencies Need to Complete Inventories and Plans to Achieve Expected Savings*, GAO-11-565 (Washington, D.C.: July 19, 2011).

[2]GAO-11-565.

[3]GAO, *GAO Schedule Assessment Guide: Best Practices for Project Schedules (Exposure Draft)*, GAO-12-120G (Washington, D.C.: May 2012).

each practice as having been fully, partially, or not addressed.[4] We
discussed our findings with agency officials to determine why the
schedules did not address all aspects of the best practices. To assess the
agencies' cost estimates, we compared documentation supporting the
cost and savings estimates found in the agencies' consolidation plans
with relevant best practices.[5] These practices include ensuring that each
estimate is comprehensive, well-documented, accurate, and credible. In
doing so, for each estimate, we rated each practice as having been met,
substantially, partially, minimally, or not met.[6] We also discussed our
findings with agency officials to determine why the estimates did not
address all aspects of the best practices. To assess the reliability of the
data the five agencies provided in their master program schedules and
cost estimates, we reviewed the schedules and estimates, compared
them to our guidance on scheduling and estimating, and interviewed
officials about how the schedules and estimates were constructed. We
concluded that the schedules and estimates were generally unreliable
and our report includes findings related to those assessments. The
results of our evaluation at these five agencies cannot be generalized to
other agencies.

To identify the key successes and challenges encountered by agencies in
consolidating data centers, we reviewed agency consolidation plans and
interviewed agency officials. We then determined which successes and
challenges were encountered most often. To assess the reliability of cost
savings data reported by Interior, we confirmed that the information was
included in the department's updated consolidation plan, which the
Interior CIO attested was assessed and determined to be accurate and
complete. In doing so, we concluded that the quality of the information
was sufficient for our purposes.

---

[4]"Fully" means the agency addressed all aspects of the practice. "Partially" means the
agency addressed some, but not all, aspects of the practice. "Not addressed" means the
agency addressed no aspects of this practice.

[5]GAO, *GAO Cost Estimating and Assessment Guide*, GAO-09-3SP (Washington, D.C.:
March 2009).

[6]"Met" means the agency provided complete evidence that satisfies the entire criterion.
"Substantially" means the agency provided evidence that satisfies a large portion of the
criterion. "Partially" means the agency provided evidence that satisfies about half of the
criterion. "Minimally" means the agency provided evidence that satisfies a small portion of
the criterion. "Not met" means the agency provided no evidence that satisfies any of the
criterion.

We conducted this performance audit from September 2011 to July 2012, in accordance with generally accepted government auditing standards. Those standards require that we plan and perform the audit to obtain sufficient, appropriate evidence to provide a reasonable basis for our findings and conclusions based on our audit objectives. We believe that the evidence obtained provides a reasonable basis for our findings and conclusions based on our audit objectives.

Appendix II: Assessment of Agencies' Completion of Key Consolidation Planning Elements, Arranged by Agency

As part of its data center consolidation initiative, OMB required 24 federal departments and agencies to submit an updated data center inventory and consolidation plan. Key elements of the inventory were to include, for each data center, information on physical servers, virtualization, IT facilities and energy, network storage, and data center information. However, 3 agencies reported their inventories based on 2010 guidance, in which case they included information for each data center on IT hardware, IT software, facilities/energy/storage, and geographic location.

Key elements of the updated plan were to include information on quantitative goals, qualitative impacts, consolidation approach, consolidation scope, timeline, performance metrics, master schedule, cost-benefit analysis, risk management, consideration of a communications plan, inventory and plan verification, consolidation progress, and cost savings.

For each of the agencies, the following sections provide a brief summary of the agencies' goal for reducing the number of data centers, and an assessment of the completeness of their inventories and plans, as compared to what we reported in 2011.[1] In the case of agencies that reported using the new inventory format, we have related the old key elements, where possible. Agencies that reported using the old format are directly compared to their previous results.

The following information describes the key that we used in tables 14 through 37 to convey the results of our assessment of the agencies' compliance with OMB's requirements for the FDCCI.

● – the agency provides complete information for this element.

◑ – the agency provides some, but not all, aspects of the element.

○ – the agency does not provide information for this element.

Department of Agriculture

Agriculture plans to consolidate from 95 data centers (40 large and 55 small) to 27 centers (8 large and 19 small) by December 2015. However, the agency's asset inventory and consolidation plan remain incomplete. In its asset inventory, the agency provides complete information for 2 key elements and provides partial information for the remaining 2 elements.

---

[1]GAO-11-565.

Additionally, in its consolidation plan, Agriculture provides complete information for 9 of the 13 elements evaluated and provides partial information for the remaining 4 elements. An Agriculture official stated that the agency is dependent on component agencies to report complete inventory information. The official also stated the agency intended to provide the missing utilization plan information, as well as greater discussion of consolidation challenges in future consolidation plan updates. Table 14 provides our assessment of Agriculture's compliance with OMB's requirements in 2010 and 2011.

Table 14: Assessment of Completeness of Agriculture's Updated Data Center Consolidation Documentation in 2010 and 2011

Key inventory element	July 2010 inventory	June 2011 update	Comments
IT software assets	◑	◑	The agency provides information on systems, but only partial information on software platforms, servers, and consolidation approach.
IT hardware and utilization	●	●	The agency provides this element.
IT facilities, energy, and storage	◑	◑	The agency provides information on construction budgets and most information for power usage and capacity information.
Geographic location	◑	●	The agency provides this element.
Key plan element	**August 2010 plan**	**September 2011 update**	
Quantitative goals	●	◑	The agency provides some information on its utilization goals, but this information is not complete.
Qualitative impacts	●	●	The agency provides this element.
Consolidation approach	●	●	The agency provides this element.
Consolidation scope	●	●	The agency provides this element.
High-level timeline	●	●	The agency provides this element.
Performance metrics	○	●	The agency provides this element.
Master program schedule	●	●	The agency provides this element.
Cost-benefit analysis	◑	●	The agency provides this element.
Risk management	●	●	The agency provides this element.
Communications plan	●	●	The agency provides this element.
Inventory/plan verification	N/A	◑	The agency provides information on plan completeness, but does not provide information on inventory completeness, the steps taken to verify the data, or any data limitations.
Consolidation progress	N/A	◑	The agency discusses progress to date and 2012 targets and considers lessons learned, but does not discuss challenges.
Cost savings	N/A	◑	The agency provides information on current and planned cost savings, but does not provide information on unexpected consolidation costs or the impact of the fiscal year 2011 enacted budget.

Source: GAO analysis of Agriculture data.

Department of Commerce

The Department of Commerce (Commerce) plans to consolidate from 55 data centers (33 large and 22 small centers) to 30 data centers (21 large and 9 small centers) by December 2015. However, Commerce's asset inventory remains incomplete, while its consolidation plan is now complete. In its asset inventory, the agency provides complete information for 3 key elements and provides partial information for the remaining 2 elements. Additionally, in its consolidation plan, Commerce provides complete information for all 13 elements evaluated. A Commerce official stated that energy information is incomplete due to the lack of metering in its facilities and the inability of data center providers to supply agency-specific energy usage and cost information. Table 15 provides our assessment of Commerce's compliance with OMB's requirements in 2010 and 2011.

Table 15: Assessment of Completeness of Commerce's Updated Data Center Consolidation Documentation in 2010 and 2011

Key inventory element	July 2010 inventory	Key inventory element	June 2011 update	Description
IT software assets	●	*[Deleted in guidance]*	N/A	Information no longer required.
IT hardware and utilization	●	Physical servers	●	The agency provides this element.
		Virtualization	●	The agency provides this element.
IT facilities, energy, and storage	◐	IT facilities, energy	◐	The agency provides information on electrical metering, power capacity, and electrical usage, but is missing data in each of these areas.
		Network storage	●	The agency provides this element.
Geographic location	●	Data center information	◐	The agency provides information on types of centers and facility closures, but provides only partial information on facilities' costs and staffing information.

Key plan element	August 2010 plan	September 2011 update	Comments
Quantitative goals	●	●	The agency provides this element.
Qualitative impacts	●	●	The agency provides this element.
Consolidation approach	●	●	The agency provides this element.
Consolidation scope	●	●	The agency provides this element.
High-level timeline	●	●	The agency provides this element.
Performance metrics	●	●	The agency provides this element.
Master program schedule	○	●	The agency provides this element.
Cost-benefit analysis	◐	●	The agency provides this element.
Risk management	●	●	The agency provides this element.
Communications plan	●	●	The agency provides this element.
Inventory/plan verification	N/A	●	The agency provides this element.
Consolidation progress	N/A	●	The agency provides this element.
Cost savings	N/A	●	The agency provides this element.

Source: GAO analysis of Commerce data.

Department of Defense

The Department of Defense (Defense) plans to consolidate from 936 data centers to 392 by December 2015. However, Defense's asset inventory and consolidation plan remain incomplete. In its asset inventory, the agency provides partial information for all 5 key elements. Additionally, in its consolidation plan, Defense provides complete information for 5 of the 13 elements evaluated, provides partial information for 3 elements, and does not provide information for 5 elements. A Defense official stated that the agency's next inventory update would include more complete information. In addition, the official stated that it was a challenge for Defense to collect all of the required information because of the scope and size of the agency's consolidation effort. Table 16 provides our assessment of Defense's compliance with OMB's requirements in 2010 and 2011.

Table 16: Assessment of Completeness of Defense's Updated Data Center Consolidation Documentation in 2010 and 2011

Key inventory element	July 2010 inventory	Key inventory element	June 2011 update	Description
IT software assets	◑	[Deleted in guidance]	N/A	Information no longer required.
IT hardware and utilization	◑	Physical servers	◑	Some component agencies provide this information, but others do not.
		Virtualization	◑	Some component agencies provide this information, but others do not.
IT facilities, energy, and storage	◑	IT facilities, energy	◑	Some component agencies provide this information, but others do not.
		Network storage	◑	Some component agencies provide this information, but others do not.
Geographic location	◑	Data center information	◑	Some component agencies provide this information, but others do not.

Key plan element	August 2010 plan	November 2011 update	Comments
Quantitative goals	◑	◑	The agency provides information on the number and size of its data centers, but provides only partial information on data center energy usage and costs, and average rack space utilization.
Qualitative impacts	●	●	The agency provides this element.
Consolidation approach	●	●	The agency provides this element.
Consolidation scope	◑	○	The agency does not provide this element.
High-level timeline	◑	○	The agency does not provide this element.
Performance metrics	◑	●	The agency provides this element.
Master program schedule	○	○	The agency does not provide this element.
Cost-benefit analysis	○	○	The agency does not provide this element.
Risk management	◑	◑	The agency discusses a risk management process, but does not reference a risk management plan for the consolidation initiative.
Communications plan	●	●	The agency provides this element.
Inventory/plan verification	N/A	●	The agency provides this element.
Consolidation progress	N/A	◑	The agency discusses progress to date, consolidation challenges, successes, and lessons learned, but does not discuss whether calendar year 2012 targets will be met.
Cost savings	N/A	○	The agency does not provide this element.

Source: GAO analysis of Defense data.

Department of Education

The Department of Education (Education) plans to consolidate from five data centers (three large and two small centers) to four data centers (three large and one small center) by December 2012. However, Education's asset inventory and consolidation plan remain incomplete. In its asset inventory, the agency provides complete information for 3 key elements and provides partial information for the remaining 2 elements. Additionally, in its consolidation plan, Education provides complete information for 8 of the 13 elements evaluated, provides partial information for 2 elements, and does not provide information for 1 element. Education officials stated that 2 elements were not applicable because of the small scope of the agency's effort. Table 17 provides our assessment of Education's compliance with OMB's requirements in 2010 and 2011.

Table 17: Assessment of Completeness of Education's Updated Data Center Consolidation Documentation in 2010 and 2011

Key inventory element	July 2010 inventory	Key inventory element	June 2011 update	Description
IT software assets	●	[Deleted in guidance]	N/A	Information no longer required.
IT hardware and utilization	◐	Physical servers	●	The agency provides this element.
		Virtualization	●	The agency provides this element.
IT facilities, energy, and storage	●	IT facilities, energy	◐	The agency provides information on electrical power metering, but only provides partial information on power capacity, usage, and cost.
		Network storage	●	The agency provides this element.
Geographic location	●	Data center information	◐	The agency provides information on data center classification and size, but does not provide information on phase of closure for its one targeted facility and does not provide staffing information for any of its facilities.

Key plan element	August 2010 plan	September 2011 update	Comments
Quantitative goals	◐	●	The agency provides this element.
Qualitative impacts	○	●	The agency provides this element.
Consolidation approach	●	●	The agency provides this element.
Consolidation scope	●	●	The agency provides this element.
High-level timeline	●	●	The agency provides this element.
Performance metrics	◐	◐	The agency provides all savings metrics, but only some utilization metrics.
Master program schedule	○	N/A	Agency officials stated this element was not applicable because of the small scope of the agency's consolidation effort.
Cost-benefit analysis	○	N/A	Agency officials stated this element was not applicable because of the small scope of the agency's consolidation effort.
Risk management	◐	●	The agency provides this element.
Communications plan	●	●	The agency provides this element.
Inventory/plan verification	N/A	●	The agency provides this element.
Consolidation progress	N/A	◐	The agency provides its goals for 2012 and considers lessons learned, but does not discuss consolidation challenges or successes.
Cost savings	N/A	○	The agency does not provide this element.

Source: GAO analysis of Education data.

Department of Energy	The Department of Energy (Energy) plans to consolidate from 56 data centers (26 large and 30 small centers) to 50 data centers (21 large and 29 small centers) by December 2015. However, Energy's asset inventory and consolidation plan remain incomplete. In its asset inventory, the agency provides complete information for 3 key elements and provides partial information for the remaining 2 elements. Additionally, in its consolidation plan, Energy provides complete information for 8 of the 13 elements evaluated, provides partial information for 3 elements, and does not provide information for 2 elements. An Energy official stated that the agency's next inventory update would include more complete information. In addition, the official stated that a risk management plan was under development and that the agency planned to work with OMB's cost model to formulate better cost and savings information. Table 18 provides our assessment of Energy's compliance with OMB's requirements in 2010 and 2011.

Table 18: Assessment of Completeness of Energy's Updated Data Center Consolidation Documentation in 2010 and 2011

Key inventory element	July 2010 inventory	Key inventory element	June 2011 update	Description
IT software assets	◑	[Deleted in guidance]	N/A	Information no longer required.
IT hardware and utilization	◑	Physical servers	●	The agency provides this element.
		Virtualization	●	The agency provides this element.
IT facilities, energy, and storage	◑	IT facilities, energy	◑	The agency provides information on electrical metering, but provides only partial information on power capacity and electricity usage.
		Network storage	●	The agency provides this element.
Geographic location	◑	Data center information	◑	The agency provides information on types of centers and facility closures, but provides only partial information on facilities' costs and staffing information.

Key plan element	August 2010 plan	September 2011 update	Comments
Quantitative goals	◑	◑	The agency provides information on the number of physical servers and the average virtualization of those servers, but does not provide information on its average server rack utilization.
Qualitative impacts	●	●	The agency provides this element.
Consolidation approach	●	●	The agency provides this element.
Consolidation scope	◑	●	The agency provides this element.
High-level timeline	○	●	The agency provides this element.
Performance metrics	○	●	The agency provides this element.
Master program schedule	○	○	The agency does not provide this element.
Cost-benefit analysis	○	○	The agency does not provide this element.
Risk management	○	◑	The agency discusses a risk management process, but does not reference a risk management plan for the consolidation initiative.
Communications plan	●	●	The agency provides this element.
Inventory/plan verification	N/A	●	The agency provides this element.
Consolidation progress	N/A	●	The agency provides this element.
Cost savings	N/A	◑	The agency provides information on current cost savings, but does not identify planned savings or the impact of the fiscal year 2011 enacted budget.

Source: GAO analysis of Energy data.

Department of Health and Human Services

The Department of Health and Human Services (HHS) plans to consolidate from 181 data centers (43 large and 138 small centers) to 145 data centers (36 large and 109 small centers) by December 2015. However, HHS's asset inventory and consolidation plan remain incomplete. In its asset inventory, the agency provides complete information for 1 key element and provides partial information for the remaining 4 elements. Additionally, in its consolidation plan, HHS provides complete information for 11 of the 13 elements evaluated and provides only partial information for the remaining 2 elements. An HHS official noted that it was difficult to gather every inventory element for all of its data centers. Table 19 provides our assessment of HHS's compliance with OMB's requirements in 2010 and 2011.

Table 19: Assessment of Completeness of HHS's Updated Data Center Consolidation Documentation in 2010 and 2011

Key inventory element	July 2010 inventory	Key inventory element	June 2011 update	Description
IT software assets	◑	*[Deleted in guidance]*	N/A	Information no longer required.
IT hardware and utilization	◑	Physical servers	◑	The agency provides full information on its types of servers, but does not provide rack count information for all of its facilities.
		Virtualization	●	The agency provides this element.
IT facilities, energy, and storage	◑	IT facilities, energy	◑	The agency provides information on its total data center power capacity and average IT electricity usage, but is missing data in each of these areas.
		Network storage	◑	The agency provides full information on its total network storage capacity, but only partial information on its use of that network storage.
Geographic location	◑	Data center information	◑	The agency provides information on its types of centers and closure information, but provides only partial information on facilities' costs and staffing information.

Key plan element	August 2010 plan	September 2011 update	Comments
Quantitative goals	◑	●	The agency provides this element.
Qualitative impacts	●	●	The agency provides this element.
Consolidation approach	●	●	The agency provides this element.
Consolidation scope	●	●	The agency provides this element.
High-level timeline	●	●	The agency provides this element.
Performance metrics	○	●	The agency provides this element.
Master program schedule	○	●	The agency provides this element.
Cost-benefit analysis	○	◑	The agency provides cost savings through 2015, but not investment costs.
Risk management	●	●	The agency provides this element.
Communications plan	●	●	The agency provides this element.
Inventory/plan verification	N/A	●	The agency provides this element.
Consolidation progress	N/A	●	The agency provides this element.
Cost savings	N/A	◑	The agency provides projected savings through 2015, but does not discuss whether there were any unexpected costs or the impact of the fiscal year 2011 enacted budget.

Source: GAO analysis of HHS data.

Department of Homeland Security	DHS plans to consolidate from 101 data centers (40 large and 61 small data centers) to 37 data centers (3 large and 34 small centers) by December 2015. However, DHS's asset inventory and consolidation plan remain incomplete. In its asset inventory, the agency provides partial information for all 5 elements. Additionally, in its consolidation plan, DHS provides complete information for 10 of the 13 elements evaluated, provides partial information for 2 elements, and does not provide information for 1 element. DHS officials stated that the completeness of inventory information has improved since 2011 and that they have developed performance metrics. They also noted that they do not expect to fully realize their cost savings until consolidation activities are complete. Table 20 provides our assessment of DHS's compliance with OMB's requirements in 2010 and 2011.

Table 20: Assessment of Completeness of DHS's Updated Data Center Consolidation Documentation in 2010 and 2011

Key inventory element	July 2010 inventory	Key inventory element	June 2011 update	Description
IT software assets	◐	*[Deleted in guidance]*	N/A	Information no longer required.
IT hardware and utilization	◐	Physical servers	◐	The agency provides information on total rack count and server types, but is missing data.
		Virtualization	◐	The agency provides information on its virtual host and virtual operating system counts, but is missing data.
IT facilities, energy, and storage	◐	IT facilities, energy	◐	The agency provides information on electrical power metering, power capacity, usage, and cost, but is missing data.
		Network storage	◐	The agency provides information on its total and used network storage, but is missing data.
Geographic location	◐	Data center information	◐	The agency provides information on its types of centers, closure information, and facilities' costs and staffing information, but is missing data.

Key plan element	August 2010 plan	September 2011 update	Comments
Quantitative goals	◐	◐	The agency provides information on its utilization goals, but partial information on its savings goals.
Qualitative impacts	●	●	The agency provides this element.
Consolidation approach	●	●	The agency provides this element.
Consolidation scope	●	●	The agency provides this element.
High-level timeline	●	●	The agency provides this element.
Performance metrics	○	○	The agency does not provide this element.
Master program schedule	●	●	The agency provides this element.
Cost-benefit analysis	●	●	The agency provides this element.
Risk management	●	●	The agency provides this element.
Communications plan	●	●	The agency provides this element.
Inventory/plan verification	N/A	●	The agency provides this element.
Consolidation progress	N/A	●	The agency provides this element.
Cost savings	N/A	◐	The agency provides information on current savings, unexpected consolidation costs, and the impact of the fiscal year 2011 enacted budget, but does not discuss future savings from fiscal year 2011 efforts.

Source: GAO analysis of DHS data.

Department of Housing and Urban Development	The Department of Housing and Urban Development (HUD) has achieved its goal of consolidation prior to the start of the FDCCI and does not plan further consolidation of its existing base of contracts. Since 2005, the agency has operated in a fully outsourced infrastructure mode with two vendors providing consolidated departmental IT operations in hosting, storage, data transport, user environments, and systems integration, with off-site disaster recovery provided by one vendor. The agency's asset inventory is complete, but its consolidation plan is not. Specifically, HUD provides complete information for 5 of the 13 elements evaluated and provides partial information for 1 element. A HUD official stated that 7 elements were not applicable because the agency has reached its consolidated end-state architecture. Table 21 provides our assessment of HUD's compliance with OMB's requirements in 2010 and 2011.

Table 21: Assessment of Completeness of HUD's Updated Data Center Consolidation Documentation in 2010 and 2011

Key inventory element	July 2010 inventory	Key inventory element	June 2011 update	Description
IT software assets	N/A	*[Deleted in guidance]*	N/A	Information no longer required.
IT hardware and utilization	N/A	Physical servers	●	The agency provides this element.
		Virtualization	●	The agency provides this element.
IT facilities, energy, and storage	N/A	IT facilities, energy	●	The agency provides this element.
		Network storage	●	The agency provides this element.
Geographic location	N/A	Data center information	●	The agency provides this element.

Key plan element	August 2010 plan	September 2011 update	Comments
Quantitative goals	N/A	N/A	An agency official stated this element was not applicable because the agency does not own or operate any data centers.
Qualitative impacts	N/A	●	The agency provides this element.
Consolidation approach	N/A	N/A	An agency official stated this element was not applicable because the agency does not own or operate any data centers.
Consolidation scope	N/A	●	The agency provides this element.
High-level timeline	N/A	●	The agency provides this element.
Performance metrics	N/A	N/A	An agency official stated this element was not applicable because the agency does not own or operate any data centers.
Master program schedule	N/A	N/A	An agency official stated this element was not applicable because the agency achieved its consolidation goals prior to the FDCCI.
Cost-benefit analysis	N/A	N/A	An agency official stated this element was not applicable because the agency achieved its consolidation goals prior to the FDCCI.
Risk management	N/A	●	The agency provides this element.
Communications plan	N/A	●	The agency provides this element.
Inventory/plan verification	N/A	◐	The agency provides information on the completeness of the consolidation plan, but does not provide information on data limitations or the steps taken to verify inventory data.
Consolidation progress	N/A	N/A	An agency official stated this element was not applicable because the agency achieved its consolidation goals prior to the FDCCI.
Cost savings	N/A	N/A	An agency official stated this element was not applicable because the agency achieved its consolidation goals prior to the FDCCI.

Source: GAO analysis of HUD data.

Department of the Interior

Interior plans to consolidate from 232 data centers (158 large and 74 small data centers) to 135 data centers (90 large and 45 small centers) by December 2015. However, Interior's asset inventory and consolidation plan remain incomplete. In its asset inventory, the agency provides complete information for 3 key elements and provides partial information for the remaining 2 elements. Additionally, in its consolidation plan, Interior provides complete information for 9 of the 13 elements evaluated, provides partial information for 3 elements, and does not provide information for 1 element. An Interior official stated that the agency expects to report more complete inventory information for the next inventory update and will report cost savings when it can more accurately estimate the agency's expected savings. Table 22 provides our assessment of Interior's compliance with OMB's requirements in 2010 and 2011.

Table 22: Assessment of Completeness of Interior's Updated Data Center Consolidation Documentation in 2010 and 2011

Key inventory element	July 2010 inventory	Key inventory element	June 2011 update	Description
IT software assets	◐	[Deleted in guidance]	N/A	Information no longer required.
IT hardware and utilization	◐	Physical servers	●	The agency provides this element.
		Virtualization	●	The agency provides this element.
IT facilities, energy, and storage	◐	IT facilities, energy	◐	The agency provides information on electrical power metering, power capacity, usage, and cost, but is missing data in each of these areas.
		Network storage	●	The agency provides this element.
Geographic location	●	Data center information	◐	The agency provides information on the size of its data centers, but only partial information on its types of centers, closure information, and facilities' costs and staffing information.

Key plan element	August 2010 plan	September 2011 update	Comments
Quantitative goals	◐	◐	The agency provides information on its savings goals, but partial information on its utilization goals.
Qualitative impacts	●	●	The agency provides this element.
Consolidation approach	●	●	The agency provides this element.
Consolidation scope	●	●	The agency provides this element.
High-level timeline	●	●	The agency provides this element.
Performance metrics	●	●	The agency provides this element.
Master program schedule	●	●	The agency provides this element.
Cost-benefit analysis	◐	◐	The agency provides information on cost estimating efforts, but does not provide information on initial investment costs or cost savings.
Risk management	●	◐	The agency discusses its risk management approach, but indicates its risk management plan has yet to be completed.
Communications plan	●	●	The agency provides this element.
Inventory/plan verification	N/A	●	The agency provides this element.
Consolidation progress	N/A	●	The agency provides this element.
Cost savings	N/A	○	The agency does not provide this element.

Source: GAO analysis of Interior data.

Department of Justice

The Department of Justice (Justice) plans to consolidate from 105 data centers (33 large and 42 small centers and 30 centers of unknown size) to 66 data centers (27 large and 39 small centers and no centers of unknown size) by December 2015. However, Justice's asset inventory and consolidation plan remain incomplete. In its asset inventory, the agency provides only partial information for all 5 key elements. Additionally, in its consolidation plan, Justice provides complete information for 10 of the 13 elements evaluated, provides partial information for 2 elements, and does not provide any information for 1 element. A Justice official stated that the agency did not know it was required to report the missing inventory information, but that the agency had the information and would include it in the next inventory update. The official did not know when the agency's savings and utilization goals would be updated. Table 23 provides our assessment of Justice's compliance with OMB's requirements in 2010 and 2011.

Table 23: Assessment of Completeness of Justice's Updated Data Center Consolidation Documentation in 2010 and 2011

Key inventory element	July 2010 inventory	Key inventory element	June 2011 update	Description
IT software assets	◐	*[Deleted in guidance]*	N/A	Information no longer required.
IT hardware and utilization	◐	Physical servers	◐	The agency provides information on its rack count and server types, but is missing data.
		Virtualization	◐	The agency provides information on its virtual host and virtual operating system counts, but is missing data.
IT facilities, energy, and storage	◐	IT facilities, energy	◐	The agency provides information on its total data center power capacity and average data center electricity usage, but is missing data.
		Network storage	◐	The agency provides information on its total and used network storage, but is missing data.
Geographic location	●	Data center information	◐	The agency provides information on facility closures, but provides only partial information on types of centers and on facilities' costs and staffing information.

Key plan element	August 2010 plan	September 2011 update	Comments
Quantitative goals	◐	○	The agency does not provide any information on savings and utilization goals.
Qualitative impacts	●	●	The agency provides this element.
Consolidation approach	●	●	The agency provides this element.
Consolidation scope	○	●	The agency provides this element.
High-level timeline	●	●	The agency provides this element.
Performance metrics	◐	●	The agency provides this element.
Master program schedule	○	●	The agency provides this element.
Cost-benefit analysis	○	◐	The agency provides information on initial projected savings, but not aggregate year-by-year information through 2015.
Risk management	●	●	The agency provides this element.
Communications plan	●	●	The agency provides this element.
Inventory/plan verification	N/A	●	The agency provides this element.
Consolidation progress	N/A	●	The agency provides this element.
Cost savings	N/A	◐	The agency provides information on 2011 savings, but does not discuss future targets, unexpected costs, or the impact of the fiscal year 2011 enacted budget.

Source: GAO analysis of Justice data.

Department of Labor

The Department of Labor (Labor) plans to consolidate from 89 data centers (20 large and 69 small centers) to 54 data centers (20 large and 34 small centers) by December 2015. However, Labor's asset inventory and consolidation plan remain incomplete. In its asset inventory, the agency provides complete information for 2 key elements and provides partial information for the remaining 3 elements. Additionally, in its consolidation plan, Labor provides complete information for 4 of the 13 elements evaluated, provides partial information for 6 elements, and does not provide information for 3 elements. A Labor official stated that the agency had difficulty obtaining energy information because of the lack of metering in its facilities. The official also noted that cost information would not be available until the end of fiscal year 2012 while savings information would not be available until fiscal year 2013. Table 24 provides our assessment of Labor's compliance with OMB's requirements in 2010 and 2011.

Table 24: Assessment of Completeness of Labor's Updated Data Center Consolidation Documentation in 2010 and 2011

Key inventory element	July 2010 inventory	Key inventory element	June 2011 update	Description
IT software assets	◑	[Deleted in guidance]	N/A	Information no longer required.
IT hardware and utilization	●	Physical servers	◑	The agency provides information on server types, but provides only partial information on total rack count.
		Virtualization	●	The agency provides this element.
IT facilities, energy, and storage	◑	IT facilities, energy	◑	The agency provides information on electrical metering, power capacity, and electrical usage, but is missing data in each of these areas.
		Network storage	●	The agency provides this element.
Geographic location	◑	Data center information	◑	The agency provides information on types of centers and facility closures, but provides only partial information on facilities' gross floor area, costs, and staffing information.

Key plan element	August 2010 plan	September 2011 update	Comments
Quantitative goals	●	◑	The agency provides its savings goals, but provides only partial information on its utilization goals.
Qualitative impacts	●	●	The agency provides this element.
Consolidation approach	●	●	The agency provides this element.
Consolidation scope	●	◑	The agency provides a list of data centers to be consolidated, but it does not identify all of the agency's planned closures.
High-level timeline	●	◑	The agency provides a high-level timeline, but it does not identify all of the agency's planned closures.
Performance metrics	○	○	The agency does not provide this element.
Master program schedule	○	○	The agency does not provide this element.
Cost-benefit analysis	◑	◑	The agency provides near-term funding availability, but does not discuss anticipated savings.
Risk management	●	●	The agency provides this element.
Communications plan	●	●	The agency provides this element.
Inventory/plan verification	N/A	◑	The agency provides information on the completeness of the consolidation plan, but does not provide information on data limitations or the steps taken to verify inventory data.
Consolidation progress	N/A	◑	The agency discusses progress meeting established consolidation goals as well as challenges, but does not discuss consolidation successes or lessons learned.
Cost savings	N/A	○	The agency does not provide this element.

Source: GAO analysis of Labor data.

Department of State

The Department of State (State) plans to consolidate from 363 data centers (12 large and 351 small data centers) to 355 data centers (4 large and 351 small centers) by December 2015. According to agency officials, the 351 small data centers are located overseas and there are no current plans to consolidate these locations because of the resulting impact on information technology operations. However, State's asset inventory and consolidation plan remain incomplete. In its asset inventory, the agency provides complete information for 1 key element and provides partial information for the remaining 4 elements. Additionally, in its consolidation plan, State provides complete information for 9 of the 13 elements evaluated, provides partial information for 3 elements, and does not provide information for 1 element. State officials stated that the agency focused on inventorying its larger domestic facilities and noted that it was difficult to capture inventory-related information, such as energy usage and costs, for its foreign posts. The officials added that State has since completed a cost-benefit analysis, the results of which would be included in the next update, and has developed detailed schedules for each year's activities. Table 25 provides our assessment of State's compliance with OMB's requirements in 2010 and 2011.

Table 25: Assessment of Completeness of State's Updated Data Center Consolidation Documentation in 2010 and 2011

Key inventory element	July 2010 inventory	Key inventory element	June 2011 update	Description
IT software assets	●	[Deleted in guidance]	N/A	Information no longer required.
IT hardware and utilization	●	Physical servers	◐	The agency provides information on server types, but only partial information on total rack count.
		Virtualization	●	The agency provides this element.
IT facilities, energy, and storage	●	IT facilities, energy	◐	The agency provides information on electrical power metering, power capacity, usage, and cost, but is missing data in each of these areas.
		Network storage	◐	The agency provides information on its total and used network storage, but is missing data in each of these areas.
Geographic location	◐	Data center information	◐	The agency provides information on types of centers and facility closures, but provides only partial information on facility staffing information.

Key plan element	August 2010 plan	September 2011 update	Comments
Quantitative goals	◐	◐	The agency provides complete information on its number of servers, but incomplete information on its data center energy usage and costs, and the average virtualization of its servers.
Qualitative impacts	●	●	The agency provides this element.
Consolidation approach	●	●	The agency provides this element.
Consolidation scope	●	●	The agency provides this element.
High-level timeline	●	●	The agency provides this element.
Performance metrics	◐	●	The agency provides this element.
Master program schedule	○	○	The agency does not provide this element.
Cost-benefit analysis	◐	◐	The agency provides cost benefit information for its domestic facilities, but does not provide information for its foreign facilities.
Risk management	●	●	The agency provides this element.
Communications plan	●	●	The agency provides this element.
Inventory/plan verification	N/A	●	The agency provides this element.
Consolidation progress	N/A	●	The agency provides this element.
Cost savings	N/A	◐	The agency provides information on unexpected consolidation costs, the impact of the fiscal year 2011 enacted budget, and current cost savings and planned savings, but does not compare the savings to targets.

Source: GAO analysis of State data.

Department of Transportation

Transportation plans to consolidate from 328 data centers (33 large and 295 small centers) to 265 data centers (24 large and 241 small centers) by December 2015. However, Transportation's asset inventory and consolidation plan remain incomplete. In its asset inventory, the agency provides complete information for 3 key elements and provides partial information for the remaining 2 elements. Additionally, in its consolidation plan, Transportation provides complete information for 8 of the 13 elements evaluated, provides partial information for 3 elements, and does not provide information for 2 elements. A Transportation official stated that the agency did not expect to see significant improvements for the energy-related information because not all facilities have meters. The official added that it was a challenge for the agency to collect inventory data for its small data centers. Table 26 provides our assessment of Transportation's compliance with OMB's requirements in 2010 and 2011.

Table 26: Assessment of Completeness of Transportation's Updated Data Center Consolidation Documentation in 2010 and 2011

Key inventory element	July 2010 inventory	Key inventory element	June 2011 update	Description
IT software assets	◑	*[Deleted in guidance]*	N/A	Information no longer required.
IT hardware and utilization	◑	Physical servers	●	The agency provides this element.
		Virtualization	●	The agency provides this element.
IT facilities, energy, and storage	◑	IT facilities, energy	◑	The agency provides information on electrical metering, but provides only partial information on power capacity and electrical usage.
		Network storage	●	The agency provides this element.
Geographic location	◑	Data center information	◑	The agency provides information on types of centers and facility closures, but provides only partial information on facilities' costs and staffing information.

Key plan element	August 2010 plan	September 2011 update	Comments
Quantitative goals	●	●	The agency provides this element.
Qualitative impacts	●	●	The agency provides this element.
Consolidation approach	●	●	The agency provides this element.
Consolidation scope	●	●	The agency provides this element.
High-level timeline	●	●	The agency provides this element.
Performance metrics	●	●	The agency provides this element.
Master program schedule	○	○	The agency does not provide this element.
Cost-benefit analysis	●	○	The agency does not provide this element.
Risk management	●	●	The agency provides this element.
Communications plan	●	●	The agency provides this element.
Inventory/plan verification	N/A	◑	The agency provides information on the completeness of the consolidation plan and data limitations, but does not discuss the steps taken to verify inventory data.
Consolidation progress	N/A	◑	The agency discusses progress to date, consolidation challenges, and the integration of lessons learned, but does not discuss consolidation successes or whether calendar year 2012 targets will be met.
Cost savings	N/A	◑	The agency provides information on current cost savings, unexpected costs, and the impact of the fiscal year 2011 enacted budget, but does not provide information on how current cost savings relate to established targets or identify future savings.

Source: GAO analysis of Transportation data.

Department of the Treasury

The Department of the Treasury (Treasury) plans to consolidate from 55 data centers (42 large and 13 small centers) to 40 data centers (29 large and 11 small centers) by December 2015. However, Treasury's asset inventory and consolidation plan remain incomplete. In its asset inventory, the agency provides complete information for 2 key elements and provides partial information for the remaining 3 elements. Additionally, in its consolidation plan, Treasury provides complete information for 6 of the 13 elements evaluated, provides partial information for 4 elements, and does not provide information for 3 elements. A Treasury official stated that installing meters to gather all inventory power information would be cost prohibitive. In addition, the official stated that the agency is working to complete the missing plan elements, including the master program schedule, risk management plan, and communications plan. Table 27 provides our assessment of Treasury's compliance with OMB's requirements in 2010 and 2011.

Table 27: Assessment of Completeness of Treasury's Updated Data Center Consolidation Documentation in 2010 and 2011

Key inventory element	July 2010 inventory	Key inventory element	June 2011 update	Description
IT software assets	◐	*[Deleted in guidance]*	N/A	Information no longer required.
IT hardware and utilization	◐	Physical servers	●	The agency provides this element.
		Virtualization	●	The agency provides this element.
IT facilities, energy, and storage	◐	IT facilities, energy	◐	The agency provides information on electrical metering, power capacity, and electrical usage, but is missing data in each of these areas.
		Network storage	◐	The agency provides information on total and used network storage, but is missing data.
Geographic location	●	Data center information	◐	The agency provides information on types of centers and facility closures, but provides only partial information on facilities' gross floor area, costs, and staffing information.

Key plan element	August 2010 plan	September 2011 update	Comments
Quantitative goals	◐	◐	The agency provides information on its numbers of servers and their average virtualization percentage, but does not provide information on data center energy usage and costs or server rack space utilization percentage.
Qualitative impacts	●	●	The agency provides this element.
Consolidation approach	●	●	The agency provides this element.
Consolidation scope	●	●	The agency provides this element.
High-level timeline	●	●	The agency provides this element.
Performance metrics	●	●	The agency provides this element.
Master program schedule	○	○	The agency does not provide this element.
Cost-benefit analysis	○	○	The agency does not provide this element.
Risk management	○	◐	The agency provides information on the tracking of risks, but does not reference a risk management plan for the consolidation initiative.
Communications plan	○	○	The agency does not provide this element.
Inventory/plan verification	N/A	●	The agency provides this element.
Consolidation progress	N/A	◐	The agency discusses progress to date, but does not discuss consolidation challenges, lessons learned, or whether calendar year 2012 targets will be met.
Cost savings	N/A	◐	The agency provides partial information on planned cost savings, and does not provide information on current savings, unexpected costs, or the impact of the fiscal year 2011 enacted budget.

Source: GAO analysis of Treasury data.

Department of Veterans Affairs

VA plans to consolidate from 97 data centers (51 large and 46 small centers) to 14 data centers (11 large and 3 small centers) by December 2015. However, VA's asset inventory and consolidation plan remain incomplete. In its asset inventory, the agency provides complete information for 3 of the key elements and provides partial information for the remaining 2 elements. Additionally, in its consolidation plan, VA provides complete information for 10 of the 13 elements evaluated, provides partial information for 2 elements, and does not provide any information for the remaining 1 element. A VA official stated that installing equipment to gather all inventory power information would be cost prohibitive. Another official stated that the agency would more fully report on cost savings in future versions of their consolidation plan. Table 28 provides our assessment of VA's compliance with OMB's requirements in 2010 and 2011.

Table 28: Assessment of Completeness of VA's Updated Data Center Consolidation Documentation in 2010 and 2011

Key inventory element	July 2010 inventory	Key inventory element	June 2011 update	Description
IT software assets	◐	[Deleted in guidance]	N/A	Information no longer required.
IT hardware and utilization	◐	Physical servers	●	The agency provides this element.
		Virtualization	●	The agency provides this element.
IT facilities, energy, and storage	◐	IT facilities, energy	◐	The agency provides information on power metering and power capacity, but provides only partial information on electricity usage.
		Network storage	●	The agency provides this element.
Geographic location	◐	Data center information	◐	The agency provides information on types of centers and facility closures, but provides only partial information on facility staffing information.

Key plan element	August 2010 plan	September 2011 update	Comments
Quantitative goals	◐	●	The agency provides this element.
Qualitative impacts	●	●	The agency provides this element.
Consolidation approach	●	●	The agency provides this element.
Consolidation scope	●	●	The agency provides this element.
High-level timeline	●	●	The agency provides this element.
Performance metrics	○	●	The agency provides this element.
Master program schedule	○	●	The agency provides this element.
Cost-benefit analysis	●	◐	The agency provides information on cost-benefit results, but does not provide information on a time frame for the savings or provide the results on a fiscal year basis.
Risk management	◐	●	The agency provides this element.
Communications plan	●	●	The agency provides this element.
Inventory/plan verification	N/A	◐	The agency provides information on the completeness of the consolidation plan, but does not provide information on the steps taken to verify inventory data.
Consolidation progress	N/A	●	The agency provides this element.
Cost savings	N/A	○	The agency does not provide this element.

Source: GAO analysis of VA data.

| Environmental Protection Agency | The Environmental Protection Agency (EPA) plans to consolidate from 78 data centers (4 large and 74 small centers) to 53 data centers (4 large and 49 small centers) by December 2015. However, EPA's asset inventory and consolidation plan remain incomplete. In its asset inventory, the agency provides complete information for 3 of the key elements and provides partial information for the remaining 2 elements. Additionally, in its consolidation plan, EPA provides complete information for 10 of the 13 elements evaluated, provides partial information for 2 elements, and does not provide any information for the remaining 1 element. An EPA official stated that the agency planned to develop energy estimates for the missing inventory information and to work with OMB's cost model to develop better cost and savings information. Table 29 provides our assessment of EPA's compliance with OMB's requirements in 2010 and 2011. |

Table 29: Assessment of Completeness of EPA's Updated Data Center Consolidation Documentation in 2010 and 2011

Key inventory element	July 2010 inventory	Key inventory element	June 2011 update	Description
IT software assets	●	[Deleted in guidance]	N/A	Information no longer required.
IT hardware and utilization	●	Physical servers	●	The agency provides this element.
		Virtualization	●	The agency provides this element.
IT facilities, energy, and storage	◐	IT facilities, energy	◐	The agency provides information on power metering, but provides only partial information on data center power capacity and electricity usage.
		Network storage	●	The agency provides this element.
Geographic location	●	Data center information	◐	The agency provides information on types of centers and facility closures, but provides only partial information on facility staffing information.

Key plan element	August 2010 plan	September 2011 update	Comments
Quantitative goals	◐	●	The agency provides this element.
Qualitative impacts	●	●	The agency provides this element.
Consolidation approach	●	●	The agency provides this element.
Consolidation scope	●	●	The agency provides this element.
High-level timeline	●	●	The agency provides this element.
Performance metrics	○	●	The agency provides this element.
Master program schedule	○	○	The agency does not provide this element.
Cost-benefit analysis	○	◐	The agency provides information on annual cost avoidances, but does not provide information on year-by-year cost investment and cost savings calculations.
Risk management	○	●	The agency provides this element.
Communications plan	●	●	The agency provides this element.
Inventory/plan verification	N/A	●	The agency provides this element.
Consolidation progress	N/A	●	The agency provides this element.
Cost savings	N/A	◐	The agency provides information on current and planned cost savings, but does not provide information on unexpected consolidation costs or the impact of the fiscal year 2011 enacted budget.

Source: GAO analysis of EPA data.

General Services
Administration

The General Services Administration (GSA) plans to consolidate from 21 data centers (21 large and no small centers) to 9 data centers (9 large and no small centers) by December 2015. However, GSA's asset inventory and consolidation plan remain incomplete. In its asset inventory, the agency provides partial information for all 5 key elements. Additionally, in its consolidation plan, GSA provides complete information for 10 of the 13 elements evaluated and provides partial information for the 3 remaining elements. A GSA official stated that the agency had now completed all missing IT facilities and energy information, but that there were continuing difficulties in calculating savings information due to changing schedules and lack of energy metering information for some GSA facilities. Table 30 provides our assessment of GSA's compliance with OMB's requirements in 2010 and 2011.

Table 30: Assessment of Completeness of GSA's Updated Data Center Consolidation Documentation in 2010 and 2011

Key inventory element	July 2010 inventory	Key inventory element	June 2011 update	Description
IT software assets	◑	[Deleted in guidance]	N/A	Information no longer required.
IT hardware and utilization	●	Physical servers	◑	The agency provides information on total rack count and server types, but is missing data in these areas.
		Virtualization	◑	The agency provides information on virtual host and total virtual operating system counts, but is missing data.
IT facilities, energy, and storage	◑	IT facilities, energy	◑	The agency provides information on electrical metering, power capacity, and electrical usage, but is missing data.
		Network storage	◑	The agency provides information on total and used network storage, but is missing data.
Geographic location	●	Data center information	◑	The agency provides information on types of centers and facility closures, but does not provide information on facility staffing.

Key plan element	August 2010 plan	September 2011 update	Comments
Quantitative goals	◑	◑	The agency provides its savings goals, but only partial information on its utilization goals.
Qualitative impacts	●	●	The agency provides this element.
Consolidation approach	●	●	The agency provides this element.
Consolidation scope	●	●	The agency provides this element.
High-level timeline	●	●	The agency provides this element.
Performance metrics	●	●	The agency provides this element.
Master program schedule	○	●	The agency provides this element.
Cost-benefit analysis	●	●	The agency provides this element.
Risk management	●	●	The agency provides this element.
Communications plan	●	●	The agency provides this element.
Inventory/plan verification	N/A	◑	The agency provides information on inventory and plan completeness, but does not provide information on steps taken to verify inventory data.
Consolidation progress	N/A	●	The agency provides this element.
Cost savings	N/A	◑	The agency provides information on current cost savings, but does not provide information on planned savings, unexpected consolidation costs, or the impact of the fiscal year 2011 enacted budget.

Source: GAO analysis of GSA data.

National Aeronautics and Space Administration

The National Aeronautics and Space Administration (NASA) plans to consolidate from 79 data centers (75 large and 4 small data centers) to 22 large data centers by December 2015. However, NASA's asset inventory and consolidation plan remain incomplete. In its asset inventory, the agency provides complete information for 3 key elements and provides partial information for the remaining 2 elements. Additionally, in its consolidation plan, NASA provides complete information for 10 of the 13 elements evaluated, provides partial information for 2 elements, and does not provide information for the remaining element. A NASA official stated that currently only one facility has power metering and, as a result, it is difficult to determine costs. The official also noted that NASA expects to reach its 2012 consolidation targets. Table 31 provides our assessment of NASA's compliance with OMB's requirements in 2010 and 2011.

Table 31: Assessment of Completeness of NASA's Updated Data Center Consolidation Documentation in 2010 and 2011

Key inventory element	July 2010 inventory	Key inventory element	June 2011 update	Description
IT software assets	○	*[Deleted in guidance]*	N/A	Information no longer required.
IT hardware and utilization	◑	Physical servers	●	The agency provides this element.
		Virtualization	●	The agency provides this element.
IT facilities, energy, and storage	◑	IT facilities, energy	◑	The agency provides partial information on power capacity and usage, but does not provide information on power metering and cost.
		Network storage	●	The agency provides this element.
Geographic location	◑	Data center information	◑	The agency provides information on center types and sizes, and facilities' phase of closure, but provides only partial facility staffing information.

Key plan element	August 2010 plan	September 2011 update	Comments
Quantitative goals	◑	●	The agency provides this element.
Qualitative impacts	●	●	The agency provides this element.
Consolidation approach	●	●	The agency provides this element.
Consolidation scope	○	●	The agency provides this element.
High-level timeline	○	●	The agency provides this element.
Performance metrics	○	●	The agency provides this element.
Master program schedule	○	●	The agency provides this element.
Cost-benefit analysis	○	○	The agency does not provide this element.
Risk management	●	●	The agency provides this element.
Communications plan	●	●	The agency provides this element.
Inventory/plan verification	N/A	●	The agency provides this element.
Consolidation progress	N/A	◑	The agency discusses progress against goals, but does not state whether 2012 targets will be met and does not discuss challenges, lessons learned, or successes.
Cost savings	N/A	◑	The agency provides information on current cost savings, but does not provide information on planned savings, unexpected consolidation costs, or the impact of the fiscal year 2011 enacted budget.

Source: GAO analysis of NASA data.

National Science Foundation	The National Science Foundation (NSF) currently has only one onsite, centrally managed data center. Since 2007, the agency has been transitioning from owning and operating a data center to the use of commercial data center services and emerging cloud computing options. The agency's plan is to complete transition of major legacy IT systems in a phased approach, with completion coinciding with the expiration of the NSF headquarters building lease, currently set for fiscal year 2014. The agency's asset inventory is complete, but its consolidation plan is not. Specifically, NSF provides complete information for 10 of the 13 elements evaluated, provides partial information for 1 element, and does not provide information for 2 elements. An NSF official stated that the agency interpreted the guidance for consolidation progress and cost savings to apply only to ongoing or completed consolidations. However, the official noted that the agency would more fully report on these elements in future versions of its consolidation plan. Table 32 provides our assessment of NSF's compliance with OMB's requirements in 2010 and 2011.

Table 32: Assessment of Completeness of NSF's Updated Data Center Consolidation Documentation in 2010 and 2011

Key inventory element	July 2010 inventory	Key inventory element	June 2011 update	Description
IT software assets	●	[Deleted in guidance]	N/A	Information no longer required.
IT hardware and utilization	●	Physical servers	●	The agency provides this element.
		Virtualization	●	The agency provides this element.
IT facilities, energy, and storage	●	IT facilities, energy	●	The agency provides this element.
		Network storage	●	The agency provides this element.
Geographic location	●	Data center information	●	The agency provides this element.

Key plan element	August 2010 plan	September 2011 update	Comments
Quantitative goals	●	●	The agency provides this element.
Qualitative impacts	●	●	The agency provides this element.
Consolidation approach	●	●	The agency provides this element.
Consolidation scope	●	●	The agency provides this element.
High-level timeline	●	●	The agency provides this element.
Performance metrics	○	●	The agency provides this element.
Master program schedule	○	○	The agency does not provide this element.
Cost-benefit analysis	●	●	The agency provides this element.
Risk management	○	●	The agency provides this element.
Communications plan	●	●	The agency provides this element.
Inventory/plan verification	N/A	●	The agency provides this element.
Consolidation progress	N/A	◑	The agency provides information on consolidation progress and the integration of lessons learned, but does not discuss consolidation challenges or successes.
Cost savings	N/A	○	The agency does not provide this element.

Source: GAO analysis of NSF data.

Nuclear Regulatory Commission

The Nuclear Regulatory Commission (NRC) plans to consolidate from three data centers (three large and no small centers) to one large data center by December 2015. However, NRC's asset inventory and consolidation plan remain incomplete. In its asset inventory, the agency provides complete information for 4 of the key elements and partial information for the remaining 1 element. Additionally, in its consolidation plan, NRC provides complete information for 8 of the 13 elements evaluated, provides partial information for 3 elements, and does not provide information for the remaining 2 elements. An NRC official stated that the agency planned to gather missing data center information and that the agency's planned single data center would be able to provide much of NRC's missing energy information. The official also stated that both performance metrics and a master program schedule have now been developed. Table 33 provides our assessment of NRC's compliance with OMB's requirements in 2010 and 2011.

Table 33: Assessment of Completeness of NRC's Updated Data Center Consolidation Documentation in 2010 and 2011

Key inventory element	July 2010 inventory	Key inventory element	June 2011 update	Description
IT software assets	●	*[Deleted in guidance]*	N/A	Information no longer required.
IT hardware and utilization	◐	Physical servers	●	The agency provides this element.
		Virtualization	●	The agency provides this element.
IT facilities, energy, and storage	●	IT facilities, energy	●	The agency provides this element.
		Network storage	●	The agency provides this element.
Geographic location	●	Data center information	◐	The agency provides information on types of centers and facility closures, but does not provide information on facility staffing.

Key plan element	August 2010 plan	September 2011 update	Comments
Quantitative goals	◐	◐	The agency provides complete information on its numbers of servers and their average virtualization percentage, but incomplete information on data center energy usage and costs.
Qualitative impacts	●	●	The agency provides this element.
Consolidation approach	●	●	The agency provides this element.
Consolidation scope	●	●	The agency provides this element.
High-level timeline	●	●	The agency provides this element.
Performance metrics	○	○	The agency does not provide this element.
Master program schedule	○	○	The agency does not provide this element.
Cost-benefit analysis	○	◐	The agency provides information on initial investment costs, but does not provide information on cost savings.
Risk management	○	●	The agency provides this element.
Communications plan	○	●	The agency provides this element.
Inventory/plan verification	N/A	●	The agency provides this element.
Consolidation progress	N/A	●	The agency provides this element.
Cost savings	N/A	◐	The agency provides information on current cost savings, but does not provide information on planned savings, unexpected consolidation costs, or the impact of the fiscal year 2011 enacted budget.

Source: GAO analysis of NRC data.

Office of Personnel Management	The Office of Personnel Management (OPM) plans to consolidate from 4 data centers (one large and three small centers) to 3 centers (one large and two small centers) by December 2015. However, the agency's asset inventory and consolidation plan remain incomplete. In its asset inventory, the agency provides complete information for 1 key element and provides partial information for the remaining 3 elements. Additionally, in its consolidation plan, OPM provides complete information for 6 of the 13 elements evaluated, provides partial information for 2 elements, and does not provide information for 3 elements. Two elements were determined to be not applicable to the agency. An OPM official stated that several missing elements, such as more detailed and complete inventory information and a summary of the agency's cost-benefit analysis would be provided in future updates. The official also stated that the agency was not aware that it had to include consolidation progress and cost savings information in its updated consolidation plan. Another OPM official indicated the agency intended to provide information required by OMB's guidance in the future. Table 34 provides our assessment of OPM's compliance with OMB's requirements in 2010 and 2011.

Table 34: Assessment of Completeness of OPM's Updated Data Center Consolidation Documentation in 2010 and 2011

Key inventory element	July 2010 inventory	June 2011 update	Comments
IT software assets	◑	◑	The agency provides information on systems and software platforms, but only partial information on servers and consolidation approach.
IT hardware and utilization	●	●	The agency provides this element.
IT facilities, energy, and storage	◑	◑	The agency provides information on data center costs, and energy usage and costs, but does not provide information on construction budget and storage capacity types.
Geographic location	◑	◑	The agency provides information on the number and size of its data centers, but is missing data.

Key plan element	August 2010 plan	September 2011 update	Comments
Quantitative goals	●	●	The agency provides this element.
Qualitative impacts	●	●	The agency provides this element.
Consolidation approach	●	●	The agency provides this element.
Consolidation scope	●	●	The agency provides this element.
High-level timeline	●	●	The agency provides this element.
Performance metrics	○	●	The agency provides this element.
Master program schedule	○	○	The agency does not provide this element.
Cost-benefit analysis	◑	◑	The agency provides partial information on its cost benefit analysis, but did not provide year-by-year investment and cost savings information.
Risk management	○	○	The agency does not provide this element.
Communications plan	○	○	The agency does not provide this element.
Inventory/plan verification	N/A	◑	The agency provides information on plan and inventory completeness, including data limitations, but does not provide information on the steps taken to verify inventory data.
Consolidation progress	N/A	N/A	This element was determined to be not applicable since the agency was unaware of the requirement.
Cost savings	N/A	N/A	This element was determined to be not applicable since the agency was unaware of the requirement.

Source: GAO analysis of OPM data.

Small Business Administration	The Small Business Administration (SBA) plans to consolidate from four large data centers to two large centers by December 2015. However, the agency's asset inventory and consolidation plan remain incomplete. In its asset inventory, the agency provides complete information for 2 key elements and provides partial information for the remaining 2 elements. Additionally, in its consolidation plan, SBA provides complete information for 6 of the 13 elements evaluated, provides partial information for 2 elements, and does not provide information for the remaining 5 elements. SBA officials stated that several missing elements, such as performance metrics, a schedule, and a risk management strategy, were either developed after the plan's completion or would be developed in the future. Table 35 provides our assessment of SBA's compliance with OMB's requirements in 2010 and 2011.

Table 35: Assessment of Completeness of SBA's Updated Data Center Consolidation Documentation in 2010 and 2011

Key inventory element	July 2010 inventory	June 2011 update	Comments
IT software assets	●	●	The agency provides this element.
IT hardware and utilization	◐	◐	The agency provides complete information on its number of servers, but provides incomplete information on server utilization and host and operating system counts.
IT facilities, energy, and storage	◐	◐	The agency provides complete information on total and used network storage, but provides incomplete information on data center power usage and capacity.
Geographic location	◐	●	The agency provides this element.
Key plan element	**August 2010 plan**	**September 2011 update**	
Quantitative goals	◐	◐	The agency provides information on its savings and utilization goals, but is missing data.
Qualitative impacts	●	●	The agency provides this element.
Consolidation approach	●	●	The agency provides this element.
Consolidation scope	●	●	The agency provides this element.
High-level timeline	●	●	The agency provides this element.
Performance metrics	○	○	The agency does not provide this element.
Master program schedule	○	○	The agency does not provide this element.
Cost-benefit analysis	○	○	The agency does not provide this element.
Risk management	○	○	The agency does not provide this element.
Communications plan	●	●	The agency provides this element.
Inventory/plan verification	N/A	●	The agency provides this element.
Consolidation progress	N/A	◐	The agency discusses progress to date and considers lessons learned, but does not discuss 2012 targets or challenges.
Cost savings	N/A	○	The agency does not provide this element.

Source: GAO analysis of SBA data.

Social Security Administration

The Social Security Administration (SSA) has two large data centers and plans to replace one of them with a new facility. The agency expects the transition to begin in February 2015 and be complete in August 2016. However, SSA's consolidation plan remains incomplete. In its asset inventory, the agency provides complete information for all 5 key elements. Additionally, in its consolidation plan, SSA provides complete information for 7 of the 13 elements evaluated, provides partial information for 4 elements, and does not provide information for the remaining 2 elements. An SSA official stated that the missing utilization plan elements and the plan verification information were unintentionally omitted and that those items would be included in the next update. Table 36 provides our assessment of SSA's compliance with OMB's requirements in 2010 and 2011.

Table 36: Assessment of Completeness of SSA's Updated Data Center Consolidation Documentation in 2010 and 2011

Key inventory element	July 2010 inventory	Key inventory element	June 2011 update	Description
IT software assets	◐	*[Deleted in guidance]*	N/A	Information no longer required.
IT hardware and utilization	◐	Physical servers	●	The agency provides this element.
		Virtualization	●	The agency provides this element.
IT facilities, energy, and storage	◐	IT facilities, energy	●	The agency provides this element.
		Network storage	●	The agency provides this element.
Geographic location	◐	Data center information	●	The agency provides this element.

Key plan element	August 2010 plan	October 2011 update	Comments
Quantitative goals	◐	◐	The agency provides information on its savings goals, but only partial information on its utilization goals.
Qualitative impacts	●	●	The agency provides this element.
Consolidation approach	●	●	The agency provides this element.
Consolidation scope	●	●	The agency provides this element.
High-level timeline	●	●	The agency provides this element.
Performance metrics	○	●	The agency provides this element.
Master program schedule	○	○	The agency does not provide this element.
Cost-benefit analysis	○	○	The agency does not provide this element.
Risk management	○	●	The agency provides this element.
Communications plan	○	●	The agency provides this element.
Inventory/plan verification	N/A	◐	The agency discusses steps taken to validate the inventory and plan data, but does not discuss inventory and plan completeness or data limitations.
Consolidation progress	N/A	◐	The agency discusses consolidation progress and 2012 targets, but only partially considers consolidation challenges and lessons learned.
Cost savings	N/A	◐	The agency provides information on current and planned cost savings, but does not provide information on how these savings relate to targets and does not discuss the impact of the fiscal year 2011 enacted budget.

Source: GAO analysis of SSA data.

U.S. Agency for International Development

The U.S. Agency for International Development (USAID) plans to consolidate from six data centers (two large and four small data centers) to two small data centers by December 2012. However, USAID's asset inventory and consolidation plan remain incomplete. In its asset inventory, the agency provides complete information for 3 key elements and provides partial information for the remaining 2 elements. Additionally, in its consolidation plan, USAID provides complete information for 7 of the 13 elements evaluated, provides partial information for 4 elements, and does not provide information for the remaining 2 elements. A USAID official stated that missing server information would be included in the next inventory update and that the agency has completed a new cost-benefit analysis and taken steps to verify its inventory data. The official also said that power-related information is difficult to obtain since the agency leases its data centers. Table 37 provides our assessment of USAID's compliance with OMB's requirements in 2010 and 2011.

Table 37: Assessment of Completeness of USAID's Updated Data Center Consolidation Documentation in 2010 and 2011

Key inventory element	July 2010 inventory	Key inventory element	June 2011 update	Description
IT software assets	●	[Deleted in guidance]	N/A	Information no longer required.
IT hardware and utilization	◐	Physical servers	◐	The agency provides information on server counts, but only provides partial information on rack counts.
		Virtualization	●	The agency provides this element.
IT facilities, energy, and storage	◐	IT facilities, energy	◐	The agency provides information on electrical power metering, but only provides partial information on power capacity and usage, and provides no information on power cost.
		Network storage	●	The agency provides this element.
Geographic location	◐	Data center information	◐	The agency provides information on the type of its facilities, but provides staffing information for only one of its facilities and only partial information on the phase of closure for its targeted facilities and facility size.

Key plan element	August 2010 plan	September 2011 update	Comments
Quantitative goals	◐	◐	The agency provides information on the number of its servers and their average virtualization percentage, but incomplete information on data center energy and operational costs.
Qualitative impacts	●	●	The agency provides this element.
Consolidation approach	●	●	The agency provides this element.
Consolidation scope	●	●	The agency provides this element.
High-level timeline	●	●	The agency provides this element.
Performance metrics	●	●	The agency provides this element.
Master program schedule	○	○	The agency does not provide this element.
Cost-benefit analysis	○	◐	The agency provides information on year-by-year consolidation investment and cost savings through 2015, but notes it needs to revise costs based on new information.
Risk management	○	●	The agency provides this element.
Communications plan	○	●	The agency provides this element.
Inventory/plan verification	N/A	◐	The agency provides partial information on the completeness of its plan and inventory data, but does not provide information on steps taken to verify the data or information on any data limitations.
Consolidation progress	N/A	◐	The agency provides consolidation progress towards current and 2012 targets, but does not discuss consolidation challenges, successes, or lessons learned.
Cost savings	N/A	○	The agency does not provide this element.

Source: GAO analysis of USAID data.

Appendix III: Comments from the Department of Agriculture

United States Department of Agriculture

Office of the Chief Information Officer

1400 Independence Avenue S.W.

Washington, DC 20250

David A. Powner
Director
Information Technology Management Issues
U.S. Government Accountability Office
441 G Street, N. W.
Washington, DC 20548

JUN 2 1 2012

Dear Mr. Powner:

The U.S. Department of Agriculture has reviewed the draft report entitled *Data Center Consolidation: Agencies Making Progress on Efforts, but Inventories and Plans Need to be Completed* (GAO-12-742) (Job Code: 311252), July 2012.

Thank you for the opportunity to respond to the GAO draft report. We Concur with the content of the report and have no comments.

For additional information, please contact Denice Lotson, Office of the Chief Information Officer Audit Liaison, at 202-720-9384.

Sincerely,

Cheryl L. Cook
Acting, Chief Information Officer

Appendix IV: Comments from the Department of Homeland Security

U.S. Department of Homeland Security
Washington, DC 20528

June 28, 2012

David A. Powner
Director, Information Technology Management Issues
441 G Street, NW
U.S. Government Accountability Office
Washington, DC 20548

Re: Draft Report GAO-12-742, "DATA CENTER CONSOLIDATION: Agencies Making
        Progress on Efforts, but Inventories and Plans Need to be Completed"

Dear Mr. Powner:

Thank you for the opportunity to review and comment on this draft report. The U.S. Department of Homeland Security (DHS) appreciates the U.S. Government Accountability Office's (GAO's) work in planning and conducting its review and issuing this report.

The Department is pleased to note GAO's recognition that agencies continue to report significant planned data center facility reductions and cost savings. As of June 2012, DHS has completed the consolidation of 12 legacy data centers to the DHS Enterprise Data Centers. Based on completion of the remaining planned migrations, the Department anticipates realizing cumulative consolidation savings/cost avoidance of $2.8 billion through Fiscal Year (FY) 2030 due to these efforts.

The draft report contained one recommendation directed at DHS with which the Department concurs. Specifically, GAO recommended that the Secretary of Homeland Security:

Recommendation: Direct component agencies and their data center consolidation program managers to implement recognized best practices when completing required program schedules and cost-benefit analyses.

Response: Concur. The DHS Office of the Chief Information Officer (OCIO) is committed to the Federal Data Center Consolidation Initiative (FDCCI) and continues to include data center consolidation as one of its High Priority Initiatives for FY 2012 and FY 2013. DHS OCIO has taken further steps to rationalize the acquisition model and to utilize existing contracts with data center vendors to implement enterprise cloud service offerings such as "Email as a Service" and "Production as a Service."

DHS OCIO acknowledges the importance of implementing industry best practices when completing required program schedules and cost-benefit analyses. DHS OCIO will coordinate with the Enterprise Data Center (EDC) vendors to implement the industry best practices associated with maintaining and updating project schedules, as appropriate. DHS

will also follow the best practices regarding cost estimates outlined in this report as legacy
sites are transitioned to the EDC.

In addition, DHS will seek to implement GAO's recommendation as we are updating and
verifying the FDCCI-driven DHS inventory and overall migration plan as required within the
bounds of the federal templates and process.

Again, thank you again for the opportunity to review and comment on this draft report.
Technical comments were previously provided under separate cover. Please feel free to
contact me if you have any questions. We look forward to working with you in the future.

Sincerely,

Jim H. Crumpacker
Director
Departmental GAO-OIG Liaison Office

2

Appendix V: Comments from the Department of the Interior

United States Department of the Interior

OFFICE OF THE SECRETARY
Washington, DC 20240

JUL 0 2 2012

Mr. David A. Powner
Director
Information Technology Management Issues
U.S. Government Accountability Office
441 G Street, N.W.
Washington, D.C. 20548

Dear Mr. Powner:

Thank you for providing the Department of the Interior the opportunity to review and comment on the draft Government Accountability Office Report entitled, *DATA CENTER CONSOLIDATION: Agencies Making Progress on Efforts, but Inventories and Plans Need to be Completed* (GAO-12-742).

The Department of the Interior (DOI) remains committed to the Federal Data Center Consolidation Initiative (FDCCI), and continues to consolidate data centers consistent per the August 30, 2010 baseline plan. Additionally, the DOI expects to re-baseline the consolidation inventories and consolidation plans as we accommodate recent Office of Management and Budget (OMB) guidance clarifying the definition of "Data Centers."

The Department of the Interior concurs with the findings and recommendations.

See enclosure for general and technical comments.

If you have any questions or need additional information, please contact Bruce Downs at (703)648-5681 or Maria Clark at (303)969-5154.

Sincerely,

Rhea Suh
Assistant Secretary
Policy, Management and Budget

Enclosure

Enclosure 1

**Department of the Interior Comments on the
Government Accountability Office (GAO) Draft Report**
*DATA CENTER CONSOLIDATION: Agencies Making Progress on Efforts, but Inventories
and Plans Need to be Completed (GAO-12-742)*

General Comments:

The Department of the Interior (DOI) concurs with the General Accounting Office (GAO) recommendation that the Office of Management and Budget (OMB) ensure agencies utilize the OMB's total cost of ownership model as a standardized planning tool across the consolidation initiative with the following caveats: The Department of the Interior has a number of ongoing initiatives that operate in parallel with, and reinforce the Federal Data Center Consolidation Initiative (FDCCI). One of these initiatives is the Information Technology Transformation initiative, which is addressing Information Technology (IT) workforce levels and opportunities for efficiencies from a broader perspective than the FDCCI. Another initiative is the implementation of our Networx contract. The Total Cost of Ownership (TCO) model does not adequately accommodate the scope of workforce and network opportunities that the DOI expects to address under these two broader initiatives, and cannot be feasibly changed to address the DOI unique requirements, therefore the DOI will be developing savings and cost-avoidance projections independent of the TCO model.

Appendix VI: Comments from the Department of Veterans Affairs

DEPARTMENT OF VETERANS AFFAIRS
WASHINGTON DC 20420

June 25, 2012

Mr. David A. Powner
Director, Information Technology
   Management Issues
U.S. Government Accountability Office
441 G Street, NW
Washington, DC 20548

Dear Mr. Powner:

The Department of Veterans Affairs (VA) has reviewed the Government Accountability Office's (GAO) draft report, *"DATA CENTER CONSOLIDATION: Agencies Making Progress on Efforts, but Inventories and Plans Need to be Completed"* (GAO-12-742) and generally agrees with GAO's conclusions.

The enclosure contains VA's comments. VA appreciates the opportunity to comment on your draft report.

Sincerely,

John R. Gingrich
Chief of Staff

Enclosures

Enclosure

Department of Veterans Affairs (VA) Comments to
Government Accountability Office (GAO) Draft Report:
*"DATA CENTER CONSOLIDATION: Agencies Making Progress on Efforts,
but Inventories and Plans Need to be Completed"*
(GAO-12-742)

GAO Recommendation: We recommend that the Secretaries of Agriculture,
Homeland Security, Interior, Transportation, and Veterans Affairs, direct their
component agencies and their data center consolidation program managers to
implement recognized best practices when completing required program schedules and
cost-benefit analyses.

VA Comments: Concur. Pending receipt of the current GAO recommended practices
for program schedules and cost-benefit analysis, VA will update the Fiscal Year (FY)
2012, 4th Quarter plan submission accordingly.

Appendix VII: Comments from the Department of Commerce

UNITED STATES DEPARTMENT OF COMMERCE
The Secretary of Commerce
Washington, D.C. 20230

June 22, 2012

Mr. David A. Powner
Director, Information Technology Management
United States Government Accountability Office
Washington, DC 20548

Dear Mr. Powner:

Thank you for the opportunity to comment on the draft report from the U.S. Government Accountability Office (GAO) entitled *Data Center Consolidation: Agencies Making Progress on Efforts, but Inventories and Plans Need to be Completed* (GAO-12-742).

We concur with the general findings as they apply to the Department of Commerce and with the specific reporting on the Commerce Data Center Consolidation Plan.

If you have any questions regarding our response, please contact Jerry Harper, Acting Director, Office of Information Technology Policy and Planning, at 202-482-0222.

Sincerely,

Rebecca M. Blank
Acting Secretary of Commerce

Department of Energy
Washington, DC 20585

July 2, 2012

Mr. David A. Powner
Director, Information Technology Management Issues
Government Accountability Office
411 G Street, NW
Washington, D.C. 20548

Dear Mr. Powner:

The Department of Energy (DOE) Office of the Chief Information Officer (OCIO) appreciates the opportunity to provide comments to the General Accountability Office's (GAO) draft report entitled *Data Center Consolidation: Agencies Making Progress on Efforts, but Inventories and Plans Need to be Completed* (GAO-12-742). We understand this audit was conducted to (1) evaluate the extent to which the 24 participating agencies updated and verified their data center inventories and plans; (2) evaluate the extent to which selected agencies have adequately completed key elements of their consolidation plans; and (3) identify agencies' notable consolidation successes and challenges.

The Department of Energy concurs with the findings reported for Energy and supports comments and discussions provided by Energy representatives on various elements of our inventory and consolidation plans.

We would like to expand on our statement on page 46 (Funding Challenges) that while Energy reported little or no budgeted funding for consolidation projects, we are actively pursuing the use of Energy Savings Performance Contracts (ESPC) to self-fund our efforts. Our Headquarters Data Center Consolidation project is currently in the Investment Grade Audit phase of the ESPC with a targeted task order award in 2012.

In addition, we would like to comment on a referenced citation located on page 14, "An OMB official attributed the change in the number of large centers reported to agencies improvements in data quality" footnote (15) references an Energy IG (IG-0865) report that cites that 520 contractor-operated data centers were not reported in our FDCCI inventory. Of the 520 data centers included in the report, 106 qualify as "large" data centers. While DOE has decided not to report contractor operated data centers in the FDCCI inventory, these data centers are subject to the reporting requirements specified in the DOE Strategic Sustainability Performance Plan (SSPP).

If you have any questions, please contact me on (202) 586-0166.

Sincerely,

Fabion F. Husson, II
Director, Corporate IT Project
Management Office

Appendix IX: Comments from the Department of Health and Human Services

DEPARTMENT OF HEALTH & HUMAN SERVICES

OFFICE OF THE SECRETARY

Assistant Secretary for Legislation
Washington, DC 20201

JUN 27 2012

David A. Powner, Director
Information Technology Management Issues
U.S. Government Accountability Office
441 G Street NW
Washington, DC 20548

Dear Mr. Powner:

Attached are comments on the U.S. Government Accountability Office's (GAO) report entitled, "Data Center Consolidation: Agencies Making Progress on Efforts, but Inventories and Plans Need to be Completed" (GAO-12-742).

The Department appreciates the opportunity to review this draft section of the report prior to publication.

Sincerely,

Jim R. Esquea
Assistant Secretary for Legislation

Attachment

**GENERAL COMMENTS OF THE DEPARTMENT OF HEALTH AND HUMAN
SERVICES (HHS) ON THE GOVERNMENT ACCOUNTABILITY OFFICE'S (GAO)
DRAFT REPORT ENTITLED, "DATA CENTER CONSOLIDATION: AGENCIES
MAKING PROGRESS ON EFFORTS, BUT INVENTORIES AND PLANS NEED TO BE
COMPLETED" (GAO-12-742)**

The Department appreciates the opportunity to comment on this draft report.

The report is an accurate depiction of the HHS 2011 data center inventory and consolidation
plan. HHS is updating the data center inventory to address incomplete elements, although
gathering data center power information is still a challenge for some data centers. Per OMB
guidance, the revised inventory submitted in July 2012 will also include "contractor owned
contractor operated" facilities. HHS will use OMB's Total Cost of Ownership (TCO) model cost
estimates in the updated cost benefit analysis.

1

Appendix X: Comments from the Department of Labor

U.S. Department of Labor Office of the Assistant Secretary
for Administration and Management
Washington, D.C. 20210

JUN 1 5 2012

Mr. David A. Powner
Director
Information Technology Management Issues
Government Accountability Office
441 G St. NW
Washington, D.C. 20548

Dear Mr. Powner:

Thank you for the opportunity to review and comment on the Draft Government Accountability
Office (GAO) Report # GAO-12-742, *Data Center Consolidation: Agencies Making Progress on
Efforts, but Inventories and Plans Need to be Completed.* We appreciate the GAO's efforts and
careful collaboration during this study.

After carefully reviewing the draft GAO report, the Department of Labor has no comments to
contribute at this time.

Should you have any questions regarding the Department's response, please contact Mr. Curtis
Turner in the Office of the Chief Information Officer at Turner.Curtis.W@dol.gov or 202-693-
4567.

Sincerely,

T. Michael Kerr
Assistant Secretary for Administration and Management,
Chief Information Officer

Appendix XI: Comments from the National Science Foundation

NATIONAL SCIENCE FOUNDATION
4201 WILSON BOULEVARD, Room 1270
ARLINGTON, VIRGINIA 22230
Tel. 703-292-8040 ~ Fax. 703-292-9040

June 26, 2012

Mr. David A. Powner
Director, Information Technology Management Issues
U.S. Government Accountability Office
441 G Street, NW
Washington, DC 20548

Dear Mr. Powner:

Thank you for the opportunity to provide comments on the draft GAO Report "Data Center Consolidation: Agencies Making Progress on Efforts, but Inventories and Plans Need to be Completed" (GAO-12-742). NSF appreciates GAO's work in assessing federal progress related to the Federal Data Center Consolidation Initiative.

NSF is pleased to note GAO's generally positive assessment of our data center consolidation plan and inventory. As described in the report, our most recent data center consolidation plan reflects improvements over the initial version, although some elements remain incomplete.

NSF generally agrees with GAO's characterization of our plan, but wishes to provide clarification about the master program schedule plan element. GAO's assessment indicates that NSF did not provide a master program schedule. However, NSF did provide GAO with our master program schedule, which is included as part of our data center plan. Although our master schedule is inherently less detailed than those of agencies and departments with multiple components, it identifies all NSF consolidation activities in the format and level of detail prescribed by OMB.

Again, thank you for the opportunity to review and comment on this draft report. We look forward to working with you on future National Science Foundation engagements. If you have any questions or concerns, please feel free to contact me at (703) 292-8100.

Sincerely,

Amy Northcutt
Chief Information Officer

Appendix XII: GAO Contact and Staff Acknowledgments

GAO Contact	David A. Powner, (202) 512-9286 or pownerd@gao.gov
Staff Acknowledgments	In addition to the contact named above, individuals making contributions to this report included Colleen Phillips (Assistant Director), Justin Booth, Kathleen Lovett Epperson, Rebecca Eyler, Dave Hinchman, Fatima Jahan, Jason Lee, John Ockay, Karen Richey, and Jessica Waselkow.

GAO's Mission	The Government Accountability Office, the audit, evaluation, and investigative arm of Congress, exists to support Congress in meeting its constitutional responsibilities and to help improve the performance and accountability of the federal government for the American people. GAO examines the use of public funds; evaluates federal programs and policies; and provides analyses, recommendations, and other assistance to help Congress make informed oversight, policy, and funding decisions. GAO's commitment to good government is reflected in its core values of accountability, integrity, and reliability.
Obtaining Copies of GAO Reports and Testimony	The fastest and easiest way to obtain copies of GAO documents at no cost is through GAO's website (www.gao.gov). Each weekday afternoon, GAO posts on its website newly released reports, testimony, and correspondence. To have GAO e-mail you a list of newly posted products, go to www.gao.gov and select "E-mail Updates."
Order by Phone	The price of each GAO publication reflects GAO's actual cost of production and distribution and depends on the number of pages in the publication and whether the publication is printed in color or black and white. Pricing and ordering information is posted on GAO's website, http://www.gao.gov/ordering.htm. Place orders by calling (202) 512-6000, toll free (866) 801-7077, or TDD (202) 512-2537. Orders may be paid for using American Express, Discover Card, MasterCard, Visa, check, or money order. Call for additional information.
Connect with GAO	Connect with GAO on Facebook, Flickr, Twitter, and YouTube. Subscribe to our RSS Feeds or E-mail Updates. Listen to our Podcasts. Visit GAO on the web at www.gao.gov.
To Report Fraud, Waste, and Abuse in Federal Programs	Contact: Website: www.gao.gov/fraudnet/fraudnet.htm E-mail: fraudnet@gao.gov Automated answering system: (800) 424-5454 or (202) 512-7470
Congressional Relations	Katherine Siggerud, Managing Director, siggerudk@gao.gov, (202) 512-4400, U.S. Government Accountability Office, 441 G Street NW, Room 7125, Washington, DC 20548
Public Affairs	Chuck Young, Managing Director, youngc1@gao.gov, (202) 512-4800 U.S. Government Accountability Office, 441 G Street NW, Room 7149 Washington, DC 20548

Please Print on Recycled Paper.

www.ingramcontent.com/pod-product-compliance
Lightning Source LLC
Chambersburg PA
CBHW081107290526
45795CB00006B/2036